the complete guide to the
cat

the complete guide to the
cat
claire bessant

BARRON'S

Main Photography by Jane Burton and Paddy Cutts

The Complete Guide to the Cat

First edition for the United States and Canada published by Barron's Educational Series, Inc., 1999.

Copyright © 1999 U.S. version, Barron's Educational Series, Inc.

All inquiries should be addressed to:
Barron's Educational Series, Inc.
250 Wireless Boulevard
Hauppauge, NY 11788
http://www.barronseduc.com

Library of Congress Catalog Card No.: 99-63679
International Standard Book No.: 0-7641-5203-3

This is a Prima Editions Book
Text and design © 1999 Prima Editions, England

For Prima Editions
Editorial Director: Roger Kean
Creative Director: Oliver Frey
Series Editor: Iain MacGregor
Copy Editor: Neil Williams
Cover Design: Keith Williams
Interior Design: Paul Chubb, Charlotte Kirby
Four-Color Separation: Prima Creative Services, England

Printed and bound in Italy by Rotolito Lombarda

Picture Credits:
COVER Animals Unlimited (five images).

AKG: 11 top left; AKG/Erich Lessing: 10 right.
Animals Unlimited: 1, 2–3, 6–7 (main and inset), 20 top, 24, 27 bottom, 29, 32 top, 44 top, 46, 47, 48 right, 49 top, 52, 53 top, 62, 64 bottom, 65 top right, 73, 80 top, 83, 84 bottom, 89 top, 89 center right, 92 top, 97 bottom, 98, 99 top, 100 top, 109 top right, 136, 137 bottom, 138–139 (inset), 140, 141 top, 142, 143, 144, 145, 146 center, 146 bottom, 147 top, 147 center top, 147 bottom, 149, 150 top, 153 top, 153 center, 155, 156, 158 top, 158 bottom left, 159 top left, 159 bottom, 160, 161, 162, 163, 164, 165, 166, 167, 168, 170, 171, 173, 174, 175, 176, 177, 182, 184, 185, 186 bottom. Chanan Photography: 61, 65 top left, 70, 72, 77 bottom, 138–139, 141 bottom left, 141 bottom right, 146 top, 147 center bottom, 148, 150 bottom left, 150 bottom right, 151, 152, 153 bottom, 154, 157, 158 bottom right, 159 top right, 169, 172, 178, 179, 180, 181, 183, 189. Andrew Sparks: 106–107 (main and inset), 112, 115 (inset), 116, 117, 119, 120, 121, 122, 123, 124, 125, 126, 127, 128, 129, 129, 130, 131, 132, 133, 134, 135, 137 top. The Stock Market: 9 bottom, 12–13 (main and inset), 22 top, 30 bottom right, 32 bottom, 34, 36, 37 bottom, 39, 40, 43 top, 45, 49 bottom, 55, 56 top, 59 bottom, 60, 65 bottom, 66–67, 71, 86. Warren Photographic/Jane Burton: 8, 10 left, 11 top right, 11 bottom, 14, 15, 16, 17, 19, 20 bottom, 21 bottom, 23, 25, 26, 27 top, 28, 30 left, 30 top right, 31, 31, 33, 35, 37 top, 38, 41, 42, 43 bottom, 44 bottom, 48 left, 50, 51, 53 bottom, 54, 56 bottom, 57, 58, 59 top, 63, 64 top, 68, 69, 74, 75, 76, 77 top, 78, 79, 80 bottom, 81, 82, 84 top, 85, 87, 88, 89 center left, 90, 91, 92 bottom, 93, 94, 95, 96, 97 top, 99 bottom, 100 bottom, 101, 102, 103, 104, 105, 108, 109 top left, 109 bottom, 110, 111, 113, 114, 115 (main), 186 top, 187, 188. Warren Photographic/Kim Taylor: 9 top, 18, 18, 21 top, 22 bottom.

contents

the
cat

above and left: *Tabby or tortoiseshell, pedigree or mongrel, cats are fascinating and beautiful. Their mysteries, physical and psychological, are a challenge to those who want to understand them.*

Evolving over millions of years, the domestic cat has only "chosen" to cohabit with man during the last three millennia, although its hunting instincts are still very close to those bigger cats in the wild.

the **bigger** picture

While the majority of this book is dedicated to our pet cat—*Felis catus*—it is helpful to consider our very special pet feline alongside some of the other members of the cat family. By looking at their special senses, their behavior, and their nutritional needs, we can understand more about our pets and also see how "domestication" has shaped them. There are 38 species of cat in the world and apart from the variation in size across the species, they are remarkably similar. Scaled up, the pet cat is not far removed from the tiger, leopard, or lion.

left: *The Scottish wildcat (Felis silvestris grampia) has a broader head and a shorter tail than the domestic cat.*

below: *The Bobcat (Felis lynx rufus) is a derivation of the lynx family. It inhabits large tracts of North America, Nova Scotia, and Mexico.*

Across the species the physical similarities of cats are quite evident—the rounded head, the agile and light-footed movement, specialized teeth and claws, a supple muscular body, and, in most cases, a spectacularly beautiful coat. Of course cats' coats have developed to suit the environment they inhabit, be it mottled forest, tall grassland, or parched savannah.

The cat species also share attributes such as a fine sense of balance, sensitive hearing, and excellent sight. Most species are solitary (except lions, which live and hunt in groups), and only come together for mating. The raising of offspring is then left to the female.

The instinct to hunt is deeply ingrained or "pre-wired" in cats—the exact hunting sequence depends on the type of habitat and prey, but the drive itself is inherited. Movement stimulates the impulse to attack but the skill of killing itself must be learned, and again different species have different approaches, depending on their prey.

Aside from the lion with its male mane, cats of all types show very little difference between the sexes apart from the male usually being a little bigger. All cats walk on their toes, which gives them a light but speedy

movement that cannot be sustained for any great distance—the cheetah is the only member of the feline family that will pursue its prey at great speed. Indeed, like all things feline, the cheetah has perfected its skills to the limit—it is faster than any other land animal. It also differs from other members of the feline family in that it does not retract its claws. In other cats the natural state is to have the claws sheathed—hence they are actually

protractile—but the cheetah needs its claws to give it dexterity on the ground as it sprints and turns.

Despite the similarities there are marked differences too. The big cats—the lion, tiger, leopard, snow leopard, clouded leopard, and jaguar have a special adaptation of the hyoid bone at the base of the tongue that gives them free movement of their vocal apparatus. These big cats are characterized by their ability to roar. They do not purr and they also tend to eat lying down, next to their prey. Our pet cat, *Felis catus*, is part of a 25-strong group entitled *Felis* that usually feed in the crouched position we are familiar with. They cannot roar because the hyoid bone is rigid, but they can perform that most feline of sounds, the purr.

domestication of the cat

What makes *Felis catus* different from other small cats? How much has "domestication" changed the cat? Looking at physical characteristics, it is clear that the pet cat differs very little from several of the other small cats, so where exactly did it come from?
By studying physical make-up, behavior,

below: *Leopards* (Panthera pardus) *are located over a large area of the globe—from Africa to the Far East—where, through time, they have developed a strong binding relationship with mankind.*

geographical data, and results of genetic profiles, scientists have concluded that *Felis catus* developed from *Felis silvestris lybica*, the African Wild Cat, which lives in a wide range of habitats across Africa. This sandy/agouti-colored cat with tabby markings is thought to be more adaptable to living around people and less fearful of human activities than other species.

Remains of cats found around settlements in Egypt date to 4000 BC and paintings and sculptures depicting cats in association with man are dated

c.1600 BC. The economy of Egypt relied on grain, and its storage would have attracted large numbers of rodents. Cats, too, would have been attracted to this bountiful supply of prey and could benefit from it if they could overcome their fear of man and approach the settlements. Consider some of the other species of cat and how elusive they are—they move quickly and silently, and flee from human contact. Scientists who try to study them may have to spend many years following paw prints and other signs to even catch a glimpse of them. So a cat that could get over its natural shyness and share space with other cats in the area (as with our groups of feral cats that congregate around a food source), and be less fearful

left: *This bronze Egyptian figurine (c.600 BC) emphasizes the key role the feline played in their culture, both as domestic pet and venerated deity.*

above: *This relief from the Egyptian Middle Kingdom (c.2040–1650 BC) demonstrates the importance placed upon the cat, seen here as belonging to the goddess Mut.*

above: *With its territory stretching from Mexico to Argentina, the Margay (Felis wiedi)—the long-tailed spotted cat—resembles a large domestic cat.*

of people, could benefit greatly from the food supply available.

Although the domestication of the dog would have probably followed similar lines, the dog has gone a great deal further down the road from the wolf than the cat has from its African ancestor. Although genetically very much wolf, the pet dog has changed in size and shape and in its behavior. Most dogs do not now complete the predatory behavior sequence of the wolf—they stop short of killing prey because they have been adapted by man to retrieve, herd, or chase. The cat,

however, is capable of the full predatory sequence from several months old. Cats have changed little in size or shape and behaviorally can revert to a feral or wild state without any problem. Selective breeding of cats has produced different breeds with modified body shapes and hair lengths, but cats can vary as much in their behavior individually as between breeds and, as ferals, they are almost identical to their wild ancestors.

What domestication has changed—and in fact seems to have reduced—is brain size and size of the adrenal glands. The adrenals produce adrenaline, the hormone at the center of the animal's "flight or fight" reaction—if the cat has become less reactive to stimuli that it would have found exceptionally fearful previously, its brain and body may not

need so much capacity to put "fight or flight" into action. Domestication has resulted in similar reduction of brain size in the dog, and canines exhibit neoteny—persistence of some juvenile behaviors into adulthood, which include barking, licking, and jumping up. In the cat, neoteny is less evident, but behaviors carried through from kittenhood include purring and kneading. Our domestic cats, even when feral, can live in groups, albeit centered around a source of food, but can tolerate each other's presence. Wild adult cats prefer a solitary existence—perhaps this is another way in which *Felis catus* has not quite grown up.

In essence, our domesticated cat has changed little from its wild cat ancestors—what it has learned to do is to live alongside man and benefit from the relationship. Man, in turn, gets bountiful rewards from this companionship, too.

left: *The Scottish Wild Cat (Felis silvestris grampia) has a shorter tail and a broader head than its domestic cousin.*

the **natural** cat

above and left: *The cuddly kitten, the cat curled up by the fireside; despite domestication, the cat retains its natural hunting instinct. How does the natural cat combine its two natures so successfully?*

The physical make-up of

the feline form is superb.

The design incorporates

perfect balance and agility

with an anatomy that has

adapted and allowed it to

survive and breed

successfully.

the
carnivorous desert dweller

Of all the carnivores, the felids are the most specialized meat-eaters—others, such as bears, will also eat vegetable matter. However, the cat thrives with very little, if any, direct ingestion of plant material. Of course, just as an herbivore such as the cow needs specialized digestive and metabolic processes to deal with converting grass to flesh or milk, the cat too has enhanced or eliminated certain biochemical mechanisms to deal with a diet rich in protein and fat, but with little carbohydrate.

meat is a must

This specialization has resulted in the loss of certain metabolic pathways that prevent the cat from using other matter for nutrition. The cat also needs proportionally more protein in its diet compared to other mammals—one reason is that certain liver enzymes that break down proteins are always functional (they are turned "on" and "off" in other animals) and so cats use some energy from protein just to fuel this process. Other mammals use most of their protein for growth and body maintenance. While an adult dog's protein requirement will drop to about one third of its requirements as a

left: *The lion is mainly a predator of the African plains, but there are some Asian lions to be found in northwest India.*

growing puppy, the kitten only needs about one-and-a-half times the protein of an adult cat because the adult level is still relatively high.

The cat also needs certain nutrients made by the metabolic processes of other animals and not available in plant material. Dogs have a range of biochemical processes that convert nutrients from plant and animal sources into what they require—for example they can convert the carotenes found in fruit and vegetables into vitamin A. The cat cannot do this and must obtain the vitamin already preformed in animal sources. Its hunting success has allowed it to become fully dependent on meat—it doesn't need to use "lower grade" sources such as vegetable matter, and indeed cannot now make use of them. Thus the cat is more than a carnivore—it is an obligate carnivore. To survive the cat *must* eat meat. Thus it has to be a successful hunter, and the drive to hunt has not been removed by domestication.

The pattern of feline hunting across the species depends on the availability and habits of prey and its size. Big cats that can bring down a buffalo may not need to hunt for days at a time, whereas smaller cats that survive on more bite-sized prey may need to hunt much more frequently. The built-in pattern of the cat's behavior will be driven by this need. This position at the top of the food chain shapes not only how a cat behaves, but also how it looks—its physical development and evolution have been built on its success at survival. Hence, when some people want their cats to be vegetarian to fit in with their own preferences or ethical beliefs, they need to consider that the cat they love for its looks and behavior is as it is because it is a carnivore—a vegetarian cat would probably have developed to look like a rabbit!

surviving in the heat

The cat's origins in Africa and its adaptations for survival in a hot climate are still evident in our pets. The cat's kidneys can produce a highly concentrated urine that enables it to conserve water—in fact meat has a high water content and cats can survive without actually having to drink very much water.

Cats are also very tolerant of heat—most owners worry about just how close their cats get to the fire or how they can sleep on top of seemingly boiling radiators. They can also walk across hot coals! Living in a hot environment may have allowed the cat to adapt to tolerate this heat—in fact, cats can tolerate a skin temperature of up to 126°F (52°C) (we cannot tolerate anything over 111°F [44°C]). While it would be acceptable to suggest that the pads of the feet are very thick and thus have no heat sensitivity, in other ways they are extremely sensitive and can detect very slight vibrations. However, the cat's nose and upper lip are highly sensitive to temperature.

The cat's special adaptation to hunting at dawn and dusk (see page 20) probably means that it stayed under cover for the hottest part of the day. Despite its resistance to heat, losing heat could have been a problem—cats only have sweat glands equivalent to ours between the pads of their feet and so lose heat by panting, or by the evaporation of saliva from the coat during grooming.

If this information on an animal was presented in a TV documentary, we would perhaps wonder at its special adaptations for survival and be interested in its natural history and behavior. If you have reached this point and have begun to see your cuddly domestic pet as something more unusual and exotic than you had previously appreciated, your journey into the fascinating world of the cat has begun.

the hunting cat

What do cats eat when they have to find their own food? What hunting strategies do they employ? How are they adapted to make the most of the environment and their physical attributes to catch enough prey to survive on?

While few domestic cats actually obtain all their food by hunting (most also scavenge), they can still be proficient hunters. The prey available to them obviously depends on the environment they inhabit—in some countries, such as Australia, they are blamed for greatly reducing the populations of some of the indigenous animals that had not previously needed to avoid predators. In Europe they live primarily on small rodents and some birds. Although the primary hunting time is dawn or dusk, cats are highly adaptable and will time expeditions around availability of prey. Very high or low temperatures also affect whether a cat will go hunting.

To hunt successfully a cat must locate prey accurately, move in as close as possible, and catch it before it has time to escape. Cats are good sprinters but they are only able to maintain sprint speed for a very short time before they tire; thus they must be able to move silently and without detection until they are close enough for a final burst of speed or a pounce—usually about six to seven feet (two meters) from their prey. They need to be able to grab the prey and hold it still enough to immobilize or kill it.

Cats usually use a sit-and-wait strategy in situations where the prey is likely to come to them—for example, outside burrows or on pathways regularly used by mice, voles, rats, or young rabbits. Small mammals are the cat's usual choice of prey, accounting for about 75 percent of catches. In North America and Europe voles are commonly taken and in North America squirrels and chipmunks are also preyed upon. Cats across the world take small mammals more often than birds. Birds are a little less predictable than small mammals, for obvious reasons, and can be hard to

above: *A typical hunting pose—body tense and still and focused on the prey ahead.*

below: *A successful hunt. The cat may take its meal to a safe spot to eat it.*

right: *Mother cats begin to teach their kittens about prey from an early age.*

capture—birds usually comprise only about 10 percent of catches. Some cats specialize in catching birds, becoming adept at mastering the three-dimensional problem they present. Birds can also be stalked if they are on the ground long enough or hop into the pounce zone of a stationary cat. Many cats increase their chances by ambushing a birdbath where large numbers of birds are constantly coming and going, and put their lightning-fast reflexes into action by grabbing birds with their paws and putting them into their mouths before rushing off to a safe place to pluck and eat their prey. Some felines also hunt invertebrates such as spiders, insects, mollusks, and crustaceans.

Once prey has been located using senses specially adapted to see and hear it (see pages 20–28), a cat usually creeps up fairly rapidly in that familiar stalking, crouching run, trying to take cover behind anything available. The cat will then often stop and take stock, its body flattened on the ground, its face, ears, eyes, head, and whiskers pointing forward in a highly charged yet controlled way.

When the position of the prey has been reassessed the cat will move forward again to a position where it can spring, using its hindquarters to push it forward. Before it pounces it may make that characteristic little wiggle of the bottom that comes from shifting from one hind foot to the other. Whether this is to prepare the muscles for the final pounce or to pinpoint the prey more accurately by moving its head slightly is still one of those feline mysteries. The final leap is usually fairly short and the cat grabs with its paws before moving with its teeth. A series of automatic reflexes help it position the prey in its mouth (see page 26) for the killing bite at the nape of the neck.

how successful are these top-of-the-chain predators?

Cats are thought to catch small mammals in about 10 percent of pounces—about once every two hours in a hunting foray. However, when necessity dictates, they can do better—female cats who need to hunt for their food to feed kittens can increase their performance threefold, catching prey every three to four pounces. One study revealed that female cats with kittens traveled faster between hunts, assessed sites more rapidly, and were more successful at actual capture, too. Having many small mouths to feed certainly increases motivation.

right: *Birds are harder to catch but some cats become adept at the three-dimensional hunt.*

a **sensory** machine
how the specialized hunter moves

Cats are very powerful creatures for their size. They have to be strong enough to take on various types and sizes of prey and sustain short bursts of speed, yet supple and agile enough to stalk quickly and quietly, to groom, to leap and jump, and to climb. The physiology of the cat has developed to give it a lethal grace, its body modified for efficient hunting.

skeleton and muscles
The skeleton and muscles of our pet cat are almost identical to the African Wild Cat *Felis silvestris lybica*. Some of the most dramatic aspects of the cat's skeleton are its dentition and the size of the eye sockets. The cat has fewer teeth than many other carnivores but its teeth have multiple

and very precise functions—some shear meat (cats don't chew), the canines hold prey and dislocate the vertebrae in the killing nape bite, and the tiny incisors at the front are used in grooming.

The cat has a long, flexible spine—more than 33 differently shaped vertebrae form a long, pliable arc along the back from the neck to the tail and are connected by highly mobile joints that can rotate easily and smoothly, giving the cat great suppleness. The muscle and ligament attachments to these also allow for greater movement than in other animals.

Another special adaptation for ease of movement occurs in its shoulder—the cat's collarbone or clavicle is very slim and does not attach to the shoulder

above: *A specially adapted collarbone and shoulder blades give the cat its ability to move with ease.*

joint in the way it does in humans, but lies unattached in the muscle. This adaptation frees the cat's shoulders to move with little restriction. Feline shoulder blades or scapulae are also reduced—unlike the human, whose shoulder blade lies flat on the back of the rib cage and moves little, the cat can swing its shoulder along with its leg, giving it great fluidity of movement. This mobility can be seen as the cat stalks prey—the shoulder blades or scapulae move up and down while the spine and head remain almost motionless. Cats can also turn their wrists, which allows them to use their paws almost like hands for climbing, grasping, swiping, and washing.

movement
The power for pouncing, jumping, leaping, or climbing lies in the cat's hindquarters. However, the cat is not an endurance machine—it relies on short bursts of energy when it pounces and would rather jump or gallop than run. The back legs also provide the propulsion for walking—the front legs actually act as brakes and balance for the "action" end of the cat. Cats walk on their toes; placing their feet neatly

left: *Powerful yet supple, the cat has a lethal grace.*

in front of each other they tiptoe along. The extra length this gives the limb allows them to lengthen their stride, touch the ground briefly with their toes, and move on again with that lightness of step we associate so much with cats.

Cats can leap up to five times their own height or six times their own length, often from a standing start. When leaping onto a high object, the powerful back legs provide the propulsion and the cat's ability to judge distance ensures it can land far enough forward to allow its back legs to land on the object, too.

Many members of the feline family are excellent climbers—making use of a skill not present in most of their prey, other predators, or competition. The leopard often drags its prey up a tree to keep it safe from hyenas and other animals who would gladly deprive it of its hard-won meal.

While domestic cats don't usually take their meals up trees, they regularly climb and enjoy the safety afforded by high refuges. The problem our domestic cats have lies not in going up, but in getting down again. The beautifully designed claw acts as an effective crampon going up, but it is of no use going down and the descent is sometimes an ungainly slide. However, some of the big cats, such as the Margay and the Clouded Leopard, which take to the trees regularly, have specialized ankle joints that can turn 180 degrees inward, allowing them to descend rapidly headfirst.

balance

Cats have an exceptional sense of balance—they saunter along high fences only an inch wide, seemingly without fear, walk along rooftops, and perch on fence posts to survey the lay of the land. Their ability to perform the equivalent of yoga on a tightrope is the result of fine-tuned coordination of physical and nervous systems. The cat's supple body allows it to move smoothly and its adapted shoulder blades and collarbones mean that it places its feet directly in

front of each other as it walks—thus walking along narrow ledges requires no special movement. Its tail can be used as a tightrope walker would use a pole, to balance and counterbalance as necessary.

However, it is the feline organ of balance, called the *vestibular apparatus*, that gives it its excellent balancing skills. The vestibular apparatus is part of the inner ear and consists of three fluid-filled semicircular canals lined with millions of tiny hairs. Movements of the cat's head cause the fluid to move around in these canals, moving the hairs and sending signals to the brain telling the cat about direction and speed of any movement. The organ also gives the cat information about its up/down orientation.

Although the system is present in most mammals, the cat has refined it to allow very accurate control of its head position. The information that is generated in the vestibular system is combined with that coming from the eyes and the muscles to control the whole body. Many of the reactions it elicits are automatic and enable the cat to respond rapidly and continuously to detailed information about its body, allowing it to maintain a fluidity of balance seemingly without effort. However, like the graceful swimming of a swan, all the action goes on unseen to produce a seamless performance.

self-righting during a fall

One of the cat's unique characteristics is its ability to land on its feet after a fall. While it is not true that the cat lands safely on every fall and from any height (many cats are injured in falls), it does have a remarkable ability to save itself by turning around in midair and landing safely on all fours, provided that the fall is not too great.

As a cat falls, it enters into an automatic sequence of events that allow it to flip over—in less than a tenth of a second information from its eyes and vestibular system set into sequence automatic movements that first turn the cat so that its head is horizontal and upright, then bring its body around. Nerves in the spine cause the back end of the body to turn around, too. The tail acts as a counterbalance to prevent overrotation and, by arching its back to absorb some of the shock of hitting the ground, the cat usually lands successfully and without injury.

controlling movement

Because the cat has such good control over its movements, it has a brain that devotes a greater portion of its workings to coordinating movement and balance than in many other animals. The part of the brain called the cerebellum brings together the information from the cat's exceptional senses and, via lightning-fast nerve messages, coordinates its movement to give superb control of its body and make it truly a top predator.

While messages may take a seemingly miniscule time to go from, say, the paw to the brain to be interpreted and coordinated with other information and sent back out to the body, this may still take too long for a rapid enough reaction. Consequently, the feline body has

developed many reactions that are reflexes—the information from, for instance, the organs of balance is relayed directly to muscles that set into motion a movement or sequence of movements that are "pre-programmed" and allow the animal to react without any loss of time for "thinking." With this extra-rapid response time to extra-sensitive signals and a specially developed body, the cat can make movements that are graceful, supple, and appear almost gravity-defying.

feline sight

Cats prey on small mammals, birds, and even the occasional fish. Whatever prey they specialize in or prefer, and whatever strategy they use, be it sitting and waiting or stalking, they must pinpoint the prey first. This is where the cat's special adaptations to its sense of sight come into their own.

Eyes are one of the cat's most beautiful and appealing features. However, they have not evolved that way to please us—while we can manipulate a cat's eye color by controlled breeding, its design has been perfected over millions of years for hunting. Behind the colorful iris there are adaptations that endow the cat with a distinct advantage over its prey during the twilight periods of dawn and dusk.

The cat has binocular vision—its eyes are located at the front of its skull and allow it to focus on an object and

left: The cat's pupil can open widely or, as here, constrict to a slit to prevent too much light from hitting the sensitive retina.

above: The beautiful feline eye is an adaptation to crepuscular (dawn and dusk) hunting.

judge distance. Additionally the cat can detect movement up to around 80 degrees in scope (prey animals usually have eyes positioned on the sides of the head so they can be on the watch for predators as they eat).

Inside the eye is the pupil—the aperture that lets light through onto the light-sensitive lining at the back of the eye called the retina. The feline pupil can open about three times as wide as the human pupil, thus letting in as much light as possible at the hunting times of dawn and dusk. The feline eye also has about three times the number of rods (the receptors that are sensitive to light) than we have. But just letting more light into the eye is not enough—the cat's eye also has a

special reflective layer at the back called the *tapetum ludium* that reflects light not absorbed by the retina when it first enters the eye, and gives it a second chance to be interpreted.

These two adaptations of the feline eye make the cat's night vision 40–50 percent better than ours. They also mean that when the cat's eye is illuminated by a camera flash or by a car headlight at night the eye glows a fluorescent greenish/gold when the light bounces off the reflective area. The principle is put to good use in the reflective studs used on roads to show motorists the way at night (actually sometimes called "cats' eyes").

A third adaptation of the feline eye is its ability to detect movement—large numbers of special cells are triggered by the movement and, as anyone who has played with a cat by pulling a toy mouse along on a piece of string can testify, the signals produced in the cat's brain trigger a predatory sequence of behavior—it just cannot resist chasing the moving object.

Of course, having eyes that are extremely sensitive to light can cause problems on bright sunny days when the light is very strong.

To make sure that the very sensitive system that has been adapted for night vision is not swamped during the day, the cat can shut its pupil down to a fine vertical slit, at the same time shutting its eyelids—the horizontal and vertical damping ensuring that only a small amount of light enters the eye. Light sensitivity also probably takes precedence over the sharpness of the image on the retina; cats may see a more "fuzzy" image than humans.

The retina is limited in size and by giving more space to rods (the receptors sensitive to light) rather than to cones (the cells that recognize color), the domestic cat probably sees some blues and greens but not reds in the same way that we do—they probably look gray. Other species of cat may also see in color—it depends on the prey they have been adapted to hunt; if it is highly colored and hunted during the

above: *Super-reflective cats' eyes look green if illuminated by artificial light at night or when caught in a camera flash.*

day, they may see the world in much the same hues as we do.

A final protection for the very important feline eye is its third eyelid—a thin flesh membrane that is usually tucked away at the corner of the eye but that can rapidly protect it. It can sometimes be seen when the cat is feeling unwell.

below: *The cat has binocular vision—its eyes' overlapping fields of view give it good depth perception.*

touch and hunting

Once a cat has pinpointed the position of its prey using its senses of sight and hearing, it must narrow the distance between them to about six feet (2 m.) to give itself a reasonable chance of catching the prey in a final dash or pounce. Cats can move quickly but only for short distances—the pounce needs to be accurate to prevent the prey from getting away in the undergrowth or flying off. To achieve this end the cat has developed a great suppleness and fluidity of movement, and lightning-fast reflexes, as outlined on page 19. But it has still other refinements absent in most carnivores that help it to deal with prey.

To understand the cat better it is useful to stand back and look at it afresh as an outstanding sensory machine. Most humans are not "in touch" with their environment to any great degree, but the cat is surrounded by a sensory "forcefield"—hairs sensitive to tiny movements and paws sensitive to vibration.

Like other mammals, the cat's body is covered with sensors that respond to touch and pressure, temperature and pain. Two different types of touch receptors tell the cat about movement and displacement of its skin or hair. Different types of nerve fibers serve down hairs (the soft hair of the undercoat) and groups of guard hairs (the outer coarser hairs of the coat),

left: *The feline head, a focus of supersenses—touch, taste, smell, sight, and hearing.*

while others are sensitive to vibration. This third type of sensor is found on the pads and can sense minute vibrations even though the pads are being squashed by the cat's weight. The pads of the foot and the nose have more touch receptors than other areas, and those on its feet give the cat information about movement across their surface, and are highly sensitive.

how claws work

The cat's claw is a much more complex structure than the human fingernail. The claws are attached to the end of the toe bones and ligaments link them together. When the cat is relaxed, resting, or walking, the claws are not visible—they are tucked into a pocket of skin so that the cat can move silently and doesn't get them caught on anything. In this way the tips stay razor sharp and are in peak condition for catching prey. If the claws were in a fixed position, like those of dogs, the tips would soon become worn down on rough surfaces.

The cat's claws are protractile rather than retractable—they are normally sheathed. When the cat wants to use its claws, one of the muscles and tendons in the foot pull the end bone of the toe forward, which automatically pushes the claw out and straightens the toe so that this weapon can be used to its full capacity.

The claws should not be thought of simply as hooks but as an elegant, sophisticated system that provides the cat with an ever-sharp set of rapiers and the quickest draw in town! The bases of the claws are also well-served with nerves—they give the cat information about the extension of the claws and their movement sideways. This means the claws are not merely inert nails used as simple weapons, they are sensitive tools that give the cat a great deal of extremely useful information in addition to their obvious use for catching and holding prey, and for climbing.

The cat can use its claws fiercely and strongly when hunting, or with great finesse, for example when it plays with us and grabs us very gently. Claws are a finely honed mechanism, which will come as no surprise to students of this top predator.

Cats need to move as silently as possible in order to get close to their prey. Not only can they tuck away

above: *The cat's head is surrounded by a sensory "forcefield" of hairs that are highly sensitive to any movement.*

their weapons but they are equipped with the equivalent of thick socks worn over shoes to muffle any sound—their pads and the hair that grows between them cushion each

step. As mentioned earlier, these cushions are very sensitive to vibration and give the cat information about the terrain it is moving over.

whiskers

A cat's whiskers are part of what makes it a cat, in human eyes. Similar hairs, called *vibrissae*, are also found above the cat's eyes, on its cheeks, and on its wrists (which look like its elbows but remember the cat walks on its toes—or perhaps we should say fingers for the front). These hairs go deep into the skin and are closely connected to the cat's nervous system. They give it information about how far, in what direction, and how frequently they move. Similar innervation occurs in the short hairs around the cat's lips.

What is so special about these *vibrissae*? Their function is to let the cat know when they are moved—indeed, if a whisker moves five nanometers (a distance 2,000 times less than the width of a human hair) the nerve at its base is activated. This degree of sensitivity means that the cat can monitor even small changes in air currents and the slightest touch.

Kittens grow whiskers before other hair and at birth they are fully functional. Cats usually have 24 whiskers above the lips, 12 on each side in four horizontal rows. These can function independently and flex backward and forward—they can be held into the face when eating or be thrown completely forward when the cat is pouncing on its prey. Watch a cat yawn and you will see

the range of movement possible for the whiskers. Similar hairs are also found at the back of the front legs and are used to gain information about prey the cat may be grasping, or perhaps when climbing.

It is said that blind cats can function very well by feeling their way around with their whiskers but are "lost" if the whiskers are cut. Professor Paul Leyhausen, a famous animal behaviorist, found that cats that were blindfolded and placed in a room with live prey could catch and kill it without difficulty. If its whiskers were cut the cat found the prey but did not kill it cleanly using the killing bite.

above: *The whiskers are highly flexible—they can be held close to the face or fan forward to "feel" prey.*

right: *The cat's high standards of hygiene and grooming ensure its coat and claws are in top condition and help maintain their sensitivity.*

Putting it all together
What has nature created these adaptations for? Consider the following scenario:

The cat is out at dusk, light is low, and it has pinpointed its prey with its exceptional hearing. Movement ahead in the grass has attracted its attention and it is moving forward to get close enough for a pounce at the source of the sound. Its acute sense of balance allows it to keep its head very still and its eyes focused on the movement, its night vision adaptations allowing it to make the most of the light where humans would be unable to. The cat creeps forward as silently as possible—it cannot look down at what it is walking on, as its eyes are focused on the prey ahead, but its sensitive pads are continuously giving it information about the ground underfoot and vibrations from other movements around it. The cat is sometimes said to be able to "hear" with its feet because they are so sensitive to vibration.

As it moves through undergrowth or long grass its whiskers extend to about twice the width of its face (about the width of its body), and the other *vibrissae* above its eyes and on its cheeks provide acute sensitivity around its head. With these sensitive "antennae" the cat can feel its way around in narrow spaces, or protect its eyes from branches as it moves toward its prey. The whiskers are so sensitive that they may be able to feel the movements in the air as it flows around objects—this allows the cat to avoid obstacles almost automatically before it can come into contact with them.

As it grabs the bird or rodent, the cat's farsightedness means that it cannot focus very well—it needs to use its other senses to help it with a very precise sequence of movements that align a canine tooth between the vertebrae at the back of the prey's neck, and so kill it quickly. Its eyes cannot focus this close up so it uses its whiskers to point forward and "feel" the prey. They can let the cat know which way the fur or feathers lie on its prey and help it to orient itself toward the head end.

When sensitive skin and hairs around the mouth come into contact with the prey, they put into action a sequence of automatic movements that turn the cat's head and position it to make the killing bite. Another set of receptors along the lips make the jaws open, and a further sequence of events fired by more receptors in the mouth trigger the bite itself. In a successful nape bite the canine tooth slips between the neck

left: *Ears pricked, eyes focused, senses on alert, the cat is ready to hunt.*

bones and severs the spinal cord—death is instantaneous. The canine teeth and claws are also sense organs in that they can tell the cat how much resistance or pressure they are experiencing. Successful hunting demands rapid reactions and these automatic movements mean that no time is lost—split seconds can mean the difference between feasting and starving.

tongue

Anyone who has been licked by a cat knows it can be quite a rough experience! The cat's tongue is another multipurpose part of the cat's anatomy—it is mobile and muscular, and its spoon-like shape makes it ideal to lap liquids.

It is covered with taste receptors to help the cat differentiate between foods and, of course, it is used for grooming. The surface of the tongue is covered with small raised knobs; those in the center are hook-shaped and backward-facing, and can act as a comb to clean and align hair as the cat grooms. They also help to hold onto prey and to lick meat off bones.

sixth sense?

All of these sensitivities enable the cat to be highly aware of its environment—they may also explain suspicions of a feline sixth sense. Cats have been reported to act strangely before severe weather events or earthquakes—they can probably detect minute vibrations or changes in ions in the air that occur during these outbursts of nature. Whatever the reason, scientists in countries prone to earthquakes take such behavior changes very seriously—they are all part of an early-warning system that helps to alert not-so-sensitive humans to an imminent disaster.

above: *The high-pitched squeaks of small mammals are detected by the cat's sensitive hearing.*

left: *Highly mobile ears allow the cat to pick up sounds from all around it as it hunts.*

above: *The cat can hear sounds higher than those detectable by dogs.*

feline hearing

Small mammals communicate in high-pitched squeaks, many of them beyond the range that the human ear can detect. As they move through the undergrowth they also make rustling noises that can be picked up by a sensitive ear. As the cat sits, taking in all the sights and sounds around it, extra muscles enable its ears to swivel through 180 degrees (together or independently), collecting sound and channeling it toward the eardrum (the

ears also have a communicative function—see page 42).

The differences it detects between the sounds in each ear enable the cat to distinguish between noises only three inches (8 cm) apart from a distance of six feet (2 m), or 16 inches (40 cm) apart from a distance of 66 feet (20 m), and this process is helped by the corrugations within the ear. In this way the cat can pinpoint prey very accurately and focus on it,

readjusting its approach to be even more accurate on the final pounce. Kittens that are learning to interpret all the sounds being received often make exaggerated head movements in an effort to pinpoint a sound source—that concentrated look with the head tilted to one side is not just for looking cute on chocolate boxes!

The cat can hear a very wide range of frequencies—indeed, the only animals with a larger range are the

horse and the porpoise. The feline hearing range spans ten-and-a-half octaves, an octave more than humans can detect, including frequencies higher than those detectable by dogs. More than 40,000 nerve fibers are present in the auditory nerve, compared to 30,000 in humans. The cat's additional hearing capacity lies at the top range of the scale—not surprising, because sounds made by feline prey lie at this end of the audio spectrum. It is almost certainly not able to detect sounds at the lower end of the human range.

Interestingly, when a cat has kittens its ability to pick up sounds at the top end of its hearing range actually improves— this helps it to find prey and to hear the alarm squeaks of its kittens. The cat's head is an amazing data-gathering and processing center. On pages 25–26 we examined another area of sensitivity not mentioned here—the whiskers. As we unravel some of the mysteries of the feline sensory system we must marvel at how such a born hunter could ever settle into the domesticated life of a pet.

the communicating cat

While most wild cats (with the exception of lions) are principally solitary animals, they do have to get together sometimes … for the survival of the species, at least! Our domestic cat is a little more sociable than some of its wilder cousins, but it is not a pack animal like the dog, which has a repertoire of behaviors that allow it to

form strong bonds and adapt to fit into a group hierarchy. Most feline communication is directed at keeping other cats away—except during times when they are looking for mates.

The domestic cat in its wildest or feral state needs to find enough food to eat—this can be achieved by hunting or by scavenging food (for example, around hotel trash cans if the cat lives in a built-up area). The feral cat in the country may have to catch all of its food—it needs a territory with enough prey for survival and, if it is female to

feed its kittens, too. It will defend this area against other cats that compete for food or, if it is male, for females in the vicinity.

However, defense is not necessarily about out-and-out war—male cats especially can fight fiercely, but they will have gone through a large number of signals and threats before the final confrontation takes place. If you can scare your opponent off you do not have to risk physical injury, which can be fatal if wounds become infected. So while cats do not have the social stratification of the dog in terms of dominance and submission in order to fit in with a group that must work as a whole for hunting and group living, in the feline world peace is maintained by threat and compromise, not for the benefit of a group but for the good of the individual.

How do cats let other cats in the area know where they are, give information about their reproductive state, or tell others to stay away? Much feline communication is done at a distance—they use urine and feces, as well as glandular secretions from various other parts of the body, to leave scent marks that not only reassure them in their own territory, but also tell other cats about their presence. They can pass on a great deal of information in this way

without ever having to meet at all.

Other long-distance messages that are vital for getting together and producing kittens involve the calling of the female cat or queen and the caterwauling of the male or tom cat. These must carry over a long distance and attract members of the opposite sex during the time when the female cat is fertile. Most other vocal communication is aimed at keeping other cats away and is used in much closer quarters, in conjunction with body language.

Close-quarters communication also involves scent, but body language is important and vocalization is used to some extent. However, cats use more vocal communication with their owners than they usually do with other cats—meowing in all its forms is used with owners in order to get them to do something, such as give attention, food, or warmth, and cats use it very successfully with their owners!

If we can understand even some of the basic signs that cats are communicating, we will begin to

right: *Much feline communication is aimed at keeping other cats away.*

understand how they are feeling. While we may never be able to understand, or perhaps even notice, some of the more subtle body language they exhibit, we can try to increase and use our knowledge to make them more content. It is also very satisfying to watch our pets and understand their emotional state, why they are behaving as they are, and to be able to influence this, if necessary.

right: *The result of successful communication—more cats!*

below: *Some body language is easy to read—the cat on the left is taking "the upper paw"; the cat on the right is not impressed!*

long-distance communication

We can look at feline communication in terms of long- and short-distance signals. Long-distance signals are aimed at cats to keep them away or, in the case of reproduction, to attract them from afar. They include scent marking and certain vocal repertoires.

sense of smell

When we considered the cat's special senses for hunting, we focused mostly on sight, hearing, and touch. However, cats also have an excellent sense of smell; in fact in order to understand feline communication we must be able to imagine a sense of smell so vivid it is the equivalent of the human sense of color sight. Our human sense of smell is not now used for hunting or finding a mate (not consciously, anyway), and we tend to forget this rich world of scent when we look at the behavior of other animals.

The cat's nose is small and neat, but it hides a complex arrangement of bones and cavities that warm and moisten air. A special area of 8–16 square inches (20–40 cm²) consisting of 200 million cells called the olfactory mucosa lines these structures. Despite humans' much larger size, the area within our noses is only half the size of the corresponding structure in cats. However, it is slightly larger in dogs—

left: *The cat's neat nose hides a labyrinth of cavities lined with smell-sensitive mucosa.*

probably because dogs use their sense of smell to hunt, as well as in their social interactions, and thus must be able to pick up tiny traces of scent from potential prey, as well as scents left by other dogs. Sensory cells within the mucosa recognize certain airborne chemicals and relay the signals to the olfactory bulb in the brain, in which a type of stimulation is associated with a certain smell.

tasting smells

Smell and taste are very closely linked—our own sense of taste can be affected if we have a cold or lose our sense of smell. However, cats are equipped with an exceptionally useful extra piece of smell/taste equipment in their sensory arsenal that allows them to "taste" smells. This sense is also present in horses and deer, and to make it work best the air has to be

right: Forcing air into its Jacobson's organ to sample scents, the cat makes a characteristic grimace called flehmening.

drawn into the mouth in a certain way called flehmening. This produces a very distinctive facial gesture where the cat pulls back its lips in a type of grimace (in horses it is much easier to see, as the horse stretches its head forward and lifts it upper lip, looking as if it is laughing), during which air is drawn into a small cigar-shaped sac situated just behind and above the front teeth. This is called Jacobson's organ or the vomeronasal organ, and it is connected to the roof of the mouth via a narrow passage.

When the cat flehmens it presses its tongue against the roof of its mouth, forcing the air through the organ, where it can concentrate the molecules it

wishes to sample, and taste/smell them, giving it a great deal more information than from just smelling. This behavior is most commonly seen in toms when they are smelling the urine of female cats in season, where the male is trying to extract as much information as possible about the female.

below: Catnip can elicit a flehmen response. There is a chemical in the plant that excites the cat, and is said to be similar to the effect of LSD on humans.

left: *Outside, the cat is highly aware of a mixture of scent signals that humans cannot detect.*

the anal area—in toms this is a highly pungent mixture obvious even to the insensitive human nose, and one of the reasons why we usually have our cats neutered! Scents left above ground level like this are not masked by other smells in the earth and can be carried on air currents to convey the message even further. The message can last up to two weeks, depending on the weather, and over this time the chemicals degrade at a fixed speed—cats can tell just when the mark was made and when that particular cat passed by.

Both male and female, neutered and unneutered animals, can and do spray, usually in the yard. Of course, those animals looking for a mate or trying to beat other rivals to a mate use this method of scent-laying the most. When cats spray they take up a very characteristic position with their tail held high, followed a quivering action accompanied by a paddling or treading motion with their back feet. A fine spray of about 1 ml of urine—a fraction of a fluid ounce—is squirted backward. Urination on the ground is primarily a bladder-emptying exercise and much larger volumes are deposited. Cats can also use feces to mark their territory (leaving feces in the open as a calling card is known as middening and is a ploy used by many animals).

Spraying is not the only means cats have of leaving a chemical message. Certain areas of skin on the cat's chin, lips, temples, neck and shoulders, and at the base of its tail have special sebaceous glands that produce an oily secretion and a scent specific to that particular cat. As the cat rubs or wipes itself on fences, gates, plants, and other objects, it smears them with some diluted scent. By rubbing its chin and mouth along twigs in the yard, raising its lip as if sneering, it anoints the stick with secretions directly from the gland

scent signals

This ability to sample smells very intensively means that scent messages can carry and convey a great deal of information about the sender. The most blatant of all scents that can be picked up over a long distance is sprayed urine (on a still day tomcat urine can be detected by another cat from more than 40 feet [12 m] away).

By squirting small amounts of urine onto vertical surfaces at nose height cats can make the best use of urine mixed with secretions from glands in

left: *A cat sprays a small volume of urine as a message or marker to itself and other cats.*

with the scent messages they leave, ensures that any tom in the area will arrive to try and be of service! Male caterwauling also travels quite a distance and lets the female know the tom is around, and tells other males that he will not stand for any competition. Strained intensity sounds like this are made by holding the mouth open and tense—usually when the cat is in an emotionally charged state.

around the mouth—this is known as bunting. Again these scents leave messages for other cats, as well as making the resident cat feel at home.

One further method of leaving scent marks is also open to the cat—when it strops its claws on a fence post it is not only sharpening its claws by pulling the blunt layer of the old nail off to reveal a new fine-pointed claw, it is also leaving a scent mark. Glands between the pads secrete a type of sweat that not only keeps the pads oiled, supple, and sensitive, but also leaves a scent marker for the cat in addition to the visual signs of scratched bark.

Next time you see your cat doing a patrol of the yard, watch carefully— you may notice it leaving all sorts of "secret" messages invisible to you but obvious to any feline in the area. It means that cats can keep out of each other's way if they want to, can avoid each other at certain times of the day (see pages 44–45), or meet up for social or reproductive reasons.

long-distance sounds

When female cats are in season or heat they advertize the fact by "calling," repeatedly making loud and strange meow-type noises. This, combined

right: *Territory must be watched over, even if it is from the comfort and safety of home.*

communicating
at close quarters

While many of the messages cats leave are meant to keep other cats as far away as possible, they also have to be able to make their feelings clear if and when other cats do come closer. The signals they use are visual—a range of postures and expressions of body language expressed to convey how they are feeling—and also involve scents that are exchanged and sampled at close quarters. Some vocal communications are also utilized, although these are primarily used by queens and kittens and, of course, between pet cats and their owners—but more of this later.

smelling of home

If this book was being written to explain human communication, we would begin with vocal and visual signals, and begin to explain the complex range of emotions that humans express in these ways. The chapter on smell and scents would be a great deal shorter than the others and would be based on more guesswork—as humans we do not react to scents much (with the exception of perfumes and aftershaves!), and usually it is almost entirely at the subconscious level.

For cats, smells are at the top of the list in terms of impact, and the right or wrong scent environment can mean the difference between a very confident and relaxed cat, and one constantly on edge. Of course, cats can recognize each other by sight, but confirmation of status is done by smell.

On pages 34–35 we looked at long-distance scent signals—those used by cats to leave messages for others to keep them away (except during reproductive cycles). However, our pet cats have developed to be able to share space, and seemingly enjoy the

right: *Close-quarters communication involves body language, scent messages, and some vocal communication.*

left: *As it grooms, the cat spreads the scent, produced by glands, all over its body.*

company of some other cats when it suits them. Although they are not pack animals like dogs, they have the ability to create a type of group scent that enables them to relax with other cats, people, and even other animals within their core territory—usually our homes. The "smell of home" is vital even to the single cat, and makes it feel secure and comfortable—the equivalent of us being surrounded by our own personal possessions, the decoration we feel happy with, and people we are familiar with.

Group-living lions use methods of creating a smell profile similar to those our pet cats use with us. They make use of the distinct individual scents that each cat produces in the various glands around its face, in the anal area, between the foot pads, and above the tail to build a cocktail of smells that is mixed by scent-marking and rubbing to include everyone in the group. This smell is instantly recognizable to others, and on meeting they react very differently than if they were meeting a strange cat without the group membership scent. If you own several cats that get on well, you will be able to watch this relaxed communication that allows the cats to make almost immediate physical contact, to sample each other's smells up close, and to check for reassurance that all is as it

should be. They are then free to exhibit behaviors that are much more kitten-like with each other (such as playing or grooming), safe in the knowledge that they will not have to be on guard, as they would with an unfamiliar cat.

How is this scent cocktail mixed and maintained? First of all the individual cat coats itself in its own perfume—its glands produce an individual scent; its own Chanel No.5, which it spreads over its entire coat during grooming. Cats groom along the direction in which their hair lies, their rough tongues separating each hair, removing dirt and parasites, and spreading oil and secretions from the various glands along each hair. By using their paws to wash their heads and faces, they spread the scent from the glands over the head and neck, then groom it further down the body using the tongue. At the tail end they work from the anal area out and downward, spreading the scent along the legs and tail.

A cat spends a lot of time grooming, so the scent is reapplied frequently and the fur kept in immaculate order. Amazingly, we are completely insensitive to these feline smells—one of the joys of cats is that to us they don't seem to smell, unlike their canine cousins who can be exceptionally unpleasant at times, even to the human

nose! However, coated with their secret feline perfume, cats are ready to indulge in a little scent swapping.

Imagine this scent is visible—a thin film of fluorescent oil spread over the cat's coat, stronger in color in the areas where the scent glands are situated around the head and tail, and lighter in color as it is spread further over the body. As the cat moves around the house and in the yard you will see it rub its body over objects, other cats, and other pets and people with which it is familiar. As it does so a little of this oil is smeared on furniture and animals. Points where the cat has a regular route or even favorite sleeping places will have stronger blobs of color scent than others. Places where the cat rubs its glands directly—for example, those glands around the mouth that are specifically anointed onto areas (bunting)—have stronger color, too. Of course, any areas where the cat has sprayed will be brightly colored, although this is usually confined to the yard.

right: *A mother cat greets and smells her kitten to make sure that all is well.*

grooming

If you are lucky enough to observe a mother cat and her kittens, watch how they greet her once they are old enough to be up and walking. As she approaches they run up to her, tails up straight and even slightly bent forward, releasing a "pocket" of scent. They meet nose-to-nose, then the queen checks under the tail, which the kittens have made very available by keeping their tails well out of the way. They may rub against her and even let their tails drape over her, mixing their scents and reassuring everyone that they are part of the group, and deserve some of the food she has caught for them.

Now watch your pet cat when you come in from a day away from home. It will walk quickly toward you, probably meow, raise its tail releasing smells from the anal area, and make itself available to be checked out. It will rub against your legs and walk backward and forward, anointing you with its smell and taking on some of yours.

Mutual or allo-grooming has a similar effect; not only does it allow cats to be groomed in those areas around the head where they cannot reach, but again it allows each cat to

sample intimately the other cat's perfume and mix in a little of its own. Using the color comparison as we did before, a mixture of colors would be visible, which then of course would be spread not only over each cat, but around the home, too. If you have several cats the patterns of color and intensity could become very complex. Bear this complex picture in mind

above: *An aggressively defensive cat reacts to a threat at close quarters.*

when you think about bringing an additional cat into the household—there are things you can do to ease a new cat in and try to encourage its acceptance (see pages 85–86). Not only is mutual grooming beneficial to

frightening the threat away or hiding from it so that it loses interest. To do this it tries to make itself look larger or smaller, depending on the ploy required at the time.

To make itself look larger the cat can erect the hair all along its back and tail, stand right up on the tips of its toes with its back arched, and turn its body sideways to the threat to give the full impact of size. At the extreme end of this scenario is the "witch's cat" posture, in which the tail is completely fluffed up like a bottle brush and held up straight—a posture more commonly seen in startled kittens.

The cat can use any of these ploys independently or in combination, depending on the degree of the threat. It can add vocal threats of spitting and growling to show that it too is dangerous to the opponent. At the other end of the spectrum the cat may want to hide away and try to disappear into the background—it hunches down close to the ground, keeping its head close to its body and

above: *Using their paws to groom, cats spread scent from their facial glands all over the head.*

each cat in terms of hygiene, but cats seem to enjoy the physical sensation (as they do when we stroke or pet them). This too reinforces bonds—it may give them the same feeling of security they felt when they were groomed by the queen as kittens (see page 53).

body language

Much feline body language may be so subtle that we do not notice it. However, there are many signs that we can pick up on that give us an idea of how the cat is feeling and of its emotions concerning other cats, animals, or situations with which it is interacting. If you have several pet cats

that get along very well you may seldom witness "outbursts" of body language because they are functioning on a much more intimate and subtle level, and do not need to express themselves in any exaggerated way. However, bring a new cat into the household, watch cats meeting in the yard, or study the seemingly mad antics of kittens and you will start to recognize the wide range of body language available to cats if they need it.

Of course, cats don't just use body language with their own species—a frightened cat automatically goes into a sequence of behavior directed at

right: *Cats don't usually meow to communicate with each other—they use the sound to elicit a response from their human caretakers.*

its ears flattened. In either case, if the cat has to move it does so very slowly, to avoid encouraging a chase, to monitor the threat very closely, and to wait for an opportunity to make a dash to safety.

Watch two male cats in a nonfriendly encounter in the yard. They may sit and stare at each other for a long time, challenging but not looking away. Many signals may pass between them, most of which humans are completely unaware of. However, one cat may decide that confrontation would not be in its best interests and may slowly leave in as dignified a manner as possible, ending the encounter.

If, however, they find themselves in close quarters either by accident or because a stare is not going to resolve the dispute, the cats approach each other very cautiously and each tries to smell the other without losing sight of its intentions. They may circle and growl, one taking the initiative to take on a more threatening role, its ears pricked but turned backward, its pupils constricted to a slit, and its whiskers "bristling." The end of its tail will twitch and sway in a low arc at the end and the cat may move forward.

The second cat must either become even more assertive or take on a more defensive role, its body curling in and down, its ears flattened, its pupils dilated, its eyes averted, and its tail held low. If it doesn't want to fight it must try to slink away or make a dash for freedom.

If the cat decides that it is going to make a stand, body language becomes even more exaggerated and the tension

goes up a notch. The aggressor must step up the threat by growling and moving forward. The defensive cat asserts itself too and its tail bends into a shape like an inverted "U" and bristles as it moves slowly sideways toward the aggressor. If the other cat continues to advance, it flattens its ears more and opens its mouth to hiss. The cats' bodies are coiled like springs, their senses strained to try a final bluff rather than actually come to blows in a physical fight that is likely to cause injury.

Once the threshold is crossed, a noisy struggle ensues, with the defensive cat on its back, its claws

bared and its back feet up and ready to defend its vulnerable stomach area. If the undercat cannot turn the tables, it has to try to disentangle itself and make a dash for safety to lick its wounds and recover its dignity.

This is obviously the most extreme form of confrontation between cats, and is a chance to see a range of body

43

hair, can be used to accentuate the cat's reactions. A frightened cat keeps them pulled back close to its face, reducing its apparent size, whereas they can be used to great effect to increase face size when required.

During courtship and mating other forms of body language come into play, which again may not be seen on a day-to-day basis—these are outlined on pages 49–50.

sounds

Vocal communication is not high in the feline league of interactive mediums. It is much more important in kittenhood between queens and their offspring (see page 54) than it is in adult life. Most vocal communication is for short distances, with the exception of the calling and caterwauling during courtship or the angry warning cries of rival toms, which are useful for night communication when visual signs are not of very much use.

Cats do not make sounds the same way we do—they can vocalize and breathe in and out at the same time, and use their tongue in a different way

above: *A well-directed hiss can stop a cat's rival in his tracks.*

language not usually in daily use. Kittens will act out all these behaviors as they play with each other (see pages 54–56), and this provides a wonderful way to study body posturing without the potential for injury that adults risk.

Within the above confrontation the communication aspects of the sense organs become obvious. The ears not only swivel around by 180 degrees but can also be pricked or flattened right down onto the head both for protection and to convey an emotion. A relaxed cat sits with its ears pricked but slightly turned back, ready to pick up sounds of threat or prey. If something begins to interest the cat it may twitch its ears to try and pick up the sound and pinpoint

it, then turn toward the sound, pricking its ears and turning them forward. An assertive or angry cat swivels its ears until the front is virtually facing backward (this move is exaggerated in some wild cats that have tufts or spots on their ears). A defensive cat flattens its ears until they are almost horizontal.

The eyes, too, are used to convey the cat's mood. Of course the pupil can be dilated or constricted in accordance with the level of light, but it is also influenced by the hormones that sweep the body at times of danger. If the cat is fearful its pupils dilate; an aggressive and assertive cat constricts its pupils.

The whiskers, too, like the cat's body

right: *Cats rub furniture to give it that safe smell of home.*

to form sounds. The sounds are made further back in the throat by pushing air at different speeds over the vocal cords stretched across the voice box. By changing tension in the throat they make shifts in the phonetic qualities of the noises.

Certain vocal patterns have been documented in cats, and individual cats may have their own personal sounds that they use with their owners, and that are adapted from kittenhood. It is useful to group the sounds that cats make into three different types—murmurs, vowels, and strained-intensity sounds.

So-called murmur sounds include purring and the little chirp cats make when they greet us. The sounds are made with a closed mouth and usually indicate contentment. Both of these sounds arise when cats are kittens, and persist into adulthood. A queen uses her purr to communicate with her nursing kittens, and by the time the kittens are two weeks old they can purr back to let her know that everything is fine—they can purr and suck at the same time. Exactly how cats manage to purr is still one of those feline secrets we have not quite unraveled. It is thought to be a vibration of the vocal cords, which are pulled by muscles in the walls of the voice box and controlled by nerves that dictate the purring rhythm. Cats purr when they sit on our laps, when they lounge on a warm and sunny windowsill, or when they groom each other. They may also purr when in pain, perhaps in an attempt to release natural pain killers in the body or just to reassure themselves.

"Meow" comes under the vowel category and is made by opening the mouth and gradually closing it as breath passes through and throat tension is altered. This category of sound is seldom used between cats but is one that they use with owners to get our attention. Cats may build up an individual repertoire with their owners—often very useful when they have trained us to respond to their pleas for comfort or food with a plaintive meow.

Most of the so-called strained intensity sounds are used when adult cats come together. They include growling, snarling, hissing or spitting, sounds of pain, and wails of females in season, and are made by holding the mouth open and tense.

Growls and snarls are used during fights. Hissing is a sound used when the cat is frightened or defensive—kittens frequently hiss if startled. The hiss is a very effective form of communication—it combines the auditory senses with a visual flash of mouth and teeth, as well as stimulating the sense of touch and smell as the hiss of air is directed at the opponent.

below: *Exactly how cats purr is still not understood, yet purring is one of those distinctive feline sounds that we love to hear.*

the **territorial** cat

We think of our cats as "territorial"—they will chase off other cats in the area with whom they are not on friendly terms. However, it is hard to define a cat's territory—we imagine a line drawn clearly around yards and houses that is exclusive to a particular cat, but territory is seldom as well defined as this. It depends on many factors, such as food availability, time of year, the number of cats in the vicinity, and the sexual status of those cats—male or female, neutered or unneutered. In general male cats have a much larger territory than females, and entire (unneutered) males the greatest of all. Instead of being discrete areas of "no entry" for other cats, territories overlap and cats may even share a core area. A cat that has successfully defended a territory may be confident enough to take on a larger area.

Wild-living or feral cats must be able to "make a living" for themselves—they protect a certain area of land in which they have a resting place or den, and an area where they can hunt—and they don't want other cats coming in and taking advantage of scarce resources. The dynamics of the feline social system can be dramatically altered if the availability of food improves—it means that the cats do not have to defend a huge territory that would have been necessary to provide them with enough wildlife to survive. The flexibility of the cat's social repertoire also means that it can live near to and interact with other cats if necessary or if it wants to—thus large colonies of feral and stray cats congregate around hotels or hospitals where waste food is available.

On pages 32–43 we outlined how cats leave messages for each other for long-distance and closer communication. Although we can "cat watch" and take note of some of their behavior, we are probably missing most of the complicated or subtle signals that are being made outside in our yards. Cats have areas that they frequent that we

left: *The farm tom may patrol a huge territory around a safe resting place.*

right: Life as an unneutered farm cat can be tough. Finding food, finding a mate, and keeping other cats away are all time- and energy-consuming tasks.

could categorize as their territory—these include our homes and yards, and some areas beyond. They also have regular walkways and paths that they use but that may not be classed as their territory.

They use their various scent languages to leave messages for other cats in the area, and also to make themselves feel "at home" and confident. These marks do not necessarily mean "no entry"—they are more likely to mean "the resident cat has the right to use this area at dawn." Rather than trying to defend an exclusive area, cats operate a kind of time- or territory-share, whereby certain cats will be able to use the space during certain times. The resident cat will probably have access to the best hunting grounds at the time when prey is out and about, and the others will have to fit in at other times. This sharing and marking system means that encounters are less frequent and do not have to end in conflict, which can be dangerous for both animals.

Of course, it also depends a great deal on where cats live—in urban and suburban areas there is huge competition for space and it would be impossible to keep out all rivals; in the rural or farm situation space is not at such a premium, and cats have much less chance of bumping into another feline around every corner. Most of our pets are neutered, have a bountiful food supply provided by loving owners, and a secure place to rest, safe from other cats—they have much less need for a large territory.

It is to the credit of the social adaptability of the cat that it can learn to live in high densities of other cats and work out a system to live by.

the resting cat

The cat has evolved to hunt intensively, eat a high-protein meal, then rest for a while. For the large wild cats an antelope may be a sufficient meal for several days; for the pet or feral cat several small meals a day are the normal pattern of eating, followed by rest. Some of this resting time is spent grooming (up to a third of your cat's waking hours), but a great deal of it (typically about half the day!) is spent in sleep, either "cat napping" or in deeper states of slumber.

sleep

Humans are influenced by circadian rhythms (an innate biological "clock"), and have a wake and sleep pattern of just over 24 hours. Cats follow a similar, although more fragmented, rhythm—rather than one period of sleep and one of wakefulness, the cat drifts in and out of sleeping and waking cycles throughout the day and night. Cats adapt the times they sleep to accommodate not only availability of

prey but also the activities or comings and goings of their owners.

Like most newborn mammals, kittens sleep 60–70 percent of the time, but unlike most mammals that do not sleep at all during the day as adults, feline adult levels of sleep remain at about 40–50 percent of total time, depending on how much "work" the cat has to do to survive.

Older cats (like older people) sleep more—at around ten years they sleep about 50–75 percent of the time, and this increases with age. Those at the top end of the age scale in their late teens are probably awake for less than a quarter of the day, overtaking even the levels of sleep required by kittens, although the old cat sleeps more lightly and wakes more easily than the kitten.

above: *As the day progresses, cats move to areas where there is more sunlight. They can tolerate heat a lot better than humans.*

left: *When a cat is in deep sleep it usually lies in a doughnut shape, and is not disturbed by light sounds.*

Cats exhibit slow-wave or quiet sleep and rapid eye movement (REM) sleep, as we do when we dream—they may be dreaming when their eyes, ears, whiskers, and paws are twitching.

The posture your cat adopts as it sleeps may give an indication of the depth of sleep it is experiencing. Sitting like a sphinx with eyes half-closed and its head balanced on its chest the cat can doze lightly, ears still twitching and alert for danger or sounds of prey. If it needs to sleep more deeply it will allow itself to become more off-guard and lie down. In deep sleep the cat is so relaxed it must lie stretched out flat or curled up in a doughnut shape, and is not disturbed by light sounds. In general an adult cat spends about a sixth of its life in deep sleep, half in light sleep and the rest of its time (about 35 percent) awake. Body posture will also be affected by temperature—the heat-seeking cat can find the smallest spot of sunlight on a windowsill and follow it around the house as the day progresses.

grooming

Most cats are meticulous about grooming their coats. By adopting a grooming routine where the whole coat is approached symmetrically and systematically using its barbed tongue and forepaws, the cat can reach parts that are difficult to reach. The forepaws are used to clean the face and behind the ears by covering each paw with saliva before wiping the "dirty" area several times in a circular motion from back to front. Grooming allows the cat to remove loose hair and parasites, and increases hair growth by stimulating the hair follicles.

Licking also stimulates glands that produce the oils that keep the coat waterproof, and allows the cat to re-ingest small amounts of vitamin D, a vitamin vital to its well-being. Evaporation of saliva from the coat is an essential way of keeping cool in hot weather—cats have few sweat glands to cool them in the way ours do, and so must rely on evaporation and panting to prevent overheating.

Grooming also has a social function—friendly cats living together use mutual grooming as part of their social bonding to create a group smell. Grooming seems to relieve tension in situations where the cat has been frightened, or where there is no way to escape a problem or frustration. It may be that the good feelings brought on by grooming are used to provide a displacement activity to help it cope with conflict. Another theory is that the emotional turmoil causes an increase in body temperature (like human blushing), and the grooming alleviates this by cooling the body. Whatever the reason, some frustrations or conflicts can result in overgrooming, or self-mutilation in extreme cases, an indication that the cat is not content.

the reproductive cat

left: *After mating the male cat will have to move fast to avoid the wrath of the female.*

The fecundity of the cat has been acknowledged throughout its history with man—it has been worshiped by some and persecuted as "wanton" by others.

Up to the age of around six months and during the months of October to December (in the Northern Hemisphere) the free-living domestic cat is usually anestrus—that is it is not in a reproductive state. This switching off of the reproductive cycle is brought about by the shortening of day length. It ensures that kittens are not born during the colder winter months when food is scarce and survival for both the pregnant queen and kittens would be questionable.

Cats used for breeding and kept indoors in warm conditions, and with artificial light, and some breeds, like Siamese, seem to breed all year around. People who work in feline rescue have also noticed that kittens of all breeds are being born very late into the autumn, although the reason for this is not known.

Male cats become sexually mature at around seven months. For both male and female kittens the exact time of maturity may depend on the time of year when they were born; kittens born early in the year may be able to

reproduce by the late summer or fall, whereas those born later may not mature until the next spring.

The cat is switched into mating behavior by increasing day length. Light that enters the eye stimulates a part of the brain called the hypothalamus, which regulates and controls the cat's daily rhythms such as eating, sleeping, and sexual activities. The increase in daylight hours affects the pituitary gland in the brain, which produces a hormone called follicle stimulating hormone (FSH).

The action of FSH is to stimulate the ovary to produce eggs and to trigger the female hormone estrogen that affects the female cat's behavior in readiness for reproduction. However, for the cat this time of heat or estrus is not one long period but many short periods (the cycle is about 14 days long) that begin when day length increases and stop when it begins to decrease (unless she becomes pregnant). The cat is referred to as being polyestrus—having many periods of estrus throughout the breeding season.

During this time the queen's behavior changes quite radically—owners of an unneutered queen may notice that she becomes more affectionate and what could be described as "flirtatious"—rubbing and rolling on the floor, chinning, and marking, and making a plaintive yet demanding rising and falling pitch known as "calling." She is trying to attract the attention of the toms in the area, who will need no encouragement to visit once they have picked up her scent, sound, and body signals. Owners who have not previously owned an unneutered female in season sometimes think that their cat is in pain and worry that her strange behaviors of rolling on the ground, stretching, and raising her hindquarters are signs of illness. These behaviors are perfectly normal in the feline search for a mate.

Several toms may congregate around the queen and, while a tom on his own territory may be more confident of winning any fight that

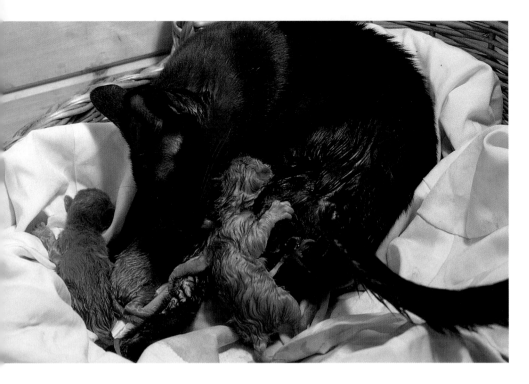

go into a period when she is non-receptive again (this can last from two days to two weeks), then the whole process repeats itself.

the pregnant queen

If mating is successful and the queen becomes pregnant, her body begins to change over the next 63 days as the fetuses grow. Very little changes outwardly in the first weeks of the pregnancy—then the hormone progesterone causes her mammary glands to swell and the nipples to become pink and more visible, and she starts to put on a little weight. She becomes progressively more rounded and heavier, and as the day of birth approaches the milk glands begin to fill.

The hormonal changes in the queen's body also bring about behavioral changes—several weeks

above: *The newborn kittens soon find a nipple and latch on to feed on colostrum—the first milk, rich in antibodies.*

might break out (and thus a chance to mate with the queen), she may have her own preferences.

The queen will not accept any advances from the males until she is ready and fully in estrus. When she is ready she exhibits what is known as the lordosis position—she puts her front end onto the ground and her rump high in the air, waving her tail around or holding it to one side. The tom mounts her and grasps her scruff, the loose skin at the back of her neck. The mating is brief and usually ends with the female "screaming" and trying to attack the male.

We do not really understand this strange behavior but it may have to do with the fact that the penis of the tom is covered in backward-facing barbs. The size of the barbs increases as male hormone (testosterone) levels rise. Whether the barbs cause pain on withdrawal is not known, but the action causes the female to ovulate, releasing eggs from the ovary to travel down the fallopian tubes and into the

two "horns" of the uterus, where fertilization occurs.

It may take several matings to stimulate ovulation, and the female may mate 10–20 times during the first day. She may mate with several toms over a period of four to six days. This sustained period of fertility gives the female a chance to mate frequently enough to ovulate but it also gives her the choice of the strongest male. A great deal of stamina is required to keep up with the demands of the female and so the successful male will probably be healthy and in his prime—giving her the best chance of having strong, healthy kittens.

It takes about two days for the eggs to reach the uterus, and the sperm remains alive for several days, moving up the vagina and into the uterus to meet the eggs. For this reason, queens can have litters that contain kittens from different fathers! When fertilized, the eggs implant in the uterus—the kitten fetuses are positioned in rows in each of the two horns of the uterus, where they develop for the next nine weeks or so.

If mating does not occur, the follicles shrivel up without releasing any eggs and the cycle is repeated. The cat will

before the birth the queen looks for a good nest site in which to hide her kittens—without the protection of a human home the safety of the kittens is far less certain. In the wild this site needs to be dry and well hidden, since it will be vital to the kittens' survival. The queen may even select several nests so she has safe alternatives should danger threaten the original site. Before the birth the queen cleans around the birth passage and the teats—it is thought that she lays a trail of saliva for the kittens to follow to find a teat after they are born.

Each kitten is born in a sac of amniotic fluid that the mother licks and nibbles at to free the kitten. She also bites through the umbilical cord and eats the kitten's placenta (it will replenish some vital nutrients and, if left, would soil the nest and attract predators and infection). Using her rough tongue she cleans the kitten's face and stimulates it to breathe.

It may take several hours for all the kittens to be born; commonly litters have four or five kittens. The queen encourages the kittens to suck, and keeps them warm by lying on her side encircling them. The kittens are guided by scent and warmth to her nipples, where they find colostrum, the first type of milk produced, which is rich in antibodies.

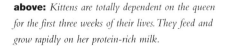

above: *Kittens are totally dependent on the queen for the first three weeks of their lives. They feed and grow rapidly on her protein-rich milk.*

learning

At birth a kitten is immature and capable of very little, yet it will have to develop exceptionally quickly—within about five months it needs to have learned how to carry out complex and coordinated behaviors in order to hunt. At birth kittens cannot control their own temperature and cannot even defecate or urinate without stimulation from their mother—she licks the urogenital area, stimulating the kitten to pass urine and feces. She eats this waste so that it does not soil the nest, preventing it from smelling, inviting infection, or predators.

Because their eyes are shut until they are about ten days old (and we are not sure how much kittens can hear initially), it is thought that they follow their heat-sensitive noses up the temperature gradient to the warm body of the queen. She lies in a crescent shape to encircle the kittens as much as possible and redirects those that crawl off in the wrong direction. Like human babies, kittens have blue eyes at birth; they start to change to their adult color at around six weeks and may not take on their full adult color until about 20 weeks.

The queen purrs while the kittens are sucking—even if they cannot hear their mother purring initially, they may be able to feel the vibrations, which again motivate them to move toward the source of nourishment. Several automatic behaviors help them to do this—a "rooting reflex" helps them nuzzle and nudge at the nipples to find them, clamp on, and stimulate milk flow, and a "sucking reflex" then takes over.

Once it has found a teat and become familiar with its position, a kitten always returns to that teat until it is weaned. Reasons for this could be to save energy that would be lost by squabbling over teats with the other kittens, and to keep a particular teat producing milk (once milk is flowing its continued production depends on continued demand—if there were only two kittens sucking a little each off six teats then milk could start to dry up).

left: *At birth kittens weigh about 3.6 ounces (100 g). This doubles in a week and triples by three weeks.*

left: *As the kittens grow, the queen offers less milk and more prey.*

right: *Kittens learn from their experiences from an early age—everything is an adventure.*

At birth a kitten weighs about 3.6 ounces (100 g), which doubles in a week and triples in three weeks— compare this to a human baby, which takes five to six months to double its birth weight. When you look at the composition of feline milk you can appreciate why—feline milk is made up of about 10 percent protein and 6 percent fat (human milk has 1 percent protein and 4 percent fat).

The kittens develop at a very rapid rate—initially they may suck for eight hours a day. Kittens can stimulate milk flow by "paddling" or treading with their paws on the queen's stomach. This is a behavior that can persist into adulthood—cats sit on our laps and purr, kneading us with apparent pleasure, or exhibit the behavior on specific textures such as woolly sweaters or sweatshirts that seem to trigger an innate reflex.

For the first two to three weeks the kittens are highly dependent on their mother, who cleans them and initiates feeding. Because they cannot regulate their own body temperature they either snuggle up to her or, if she is out hunting, snuggle together in a pile of warm kittens. If they become separated from their mother they cry loudly and the queen will come and find them. By three weeks old kittens are the equivalent of an 18-month-old baby.

Kittens start to learn to groom at about three weeks old—up until this point their mother has kept them clean and dry. By six weeks they are grooming both themselves and each other. Not only is it an essential behavior in terms of hygiene, the grooming is important for bonding relationships, and is usually

accompanied by purring. The kittens may also begin to lick their mother—this mutual grooming is another behavior that persists into adulthood and is used to cement relationships between cats.

As they approach four weeks old, kittens start to bat objects around themselves with their paws and to deposit urine and feces outside the nest as they explore—they automatically start to dig and paw at a soft substrate such as sand, soil, or litter, and will watch their mother, learning what to do and imitating her movements. They also begin to follow her around and try to explore their surroundings. By this time it is the kittens who initiate sucking—once one kitten starts, the queen begins to purr, and it is a signal for everyone to join in. The kittens can suck and purr at the same time, signaling that all is well, and the queen can use the same sound to reassure them.

above: *Learning is all about finding your limits—it can be a dangerous game, too!*

The kitten's second month of life can be compared with human childhood—it begins to play and explore and to initiate interactions. Play is a very curious behavior—most mammals play in their early development, and its importance is becoming more evident; in man we are coming to understand its value in learning and maturing, not only as practice for things we may have to do in later life, but in terms of learning to concentrate, maintaining rewarding relationships, and improving coordination.

Play begins at about four weeks and allows kittens to learn how to make judgments about what their bodies can do, estimate distances, learn about physical forces, and take chances. It allows them to try out their developing specialized senses and experiment with objects and each other. Sight is almost fully developed at

left: *For the pet cat, finding out that people are a large and important part of life is vital.*

left: *Kittens start to take an interest in solid food from the time they are about four weeks old.*

about four weeks, so the kitten can judge distance and depth reasonably accurately, and continue to perfect it until it is about four months old.

To begin with, play is fairly random, with no particular behavior sequence. However, as kittens mature, behavior starts to follow particular patterns as the nervous system develops and hunting and communication skills become evident. As this happens "play" becomes more organized and less "playful." Particular behaviors can be seen to develop as kittens grow—at four weeks they practice stand-up and belly-up positions, by week five they learn to pounce, and by week six they can chase and leap.

Grooming is also well developed from five weeks, and kittens can look after their own coats rather than rely on their mother for care. The righting reflex (see page 19) is present from about six weeks.

As these behaviors are developing, the kitten's mother starts to wean them, making herself less available and redirecting their hunger and energy to looking for solid food. At six weeks she does not lie down to let them feed but starts to walk away—by this time the

above: *As with many animals, including humans, play is a vital part of development. Kittens love it!*

above: *Once they are mobile, there's no stopping kittens from exploring their environment.*

kittens' teeth, which began to erupt at two weeks old, are sharp and painful to the mother. If she is a pet cat they will watch her eat from her bowl and follow her and experiment with the food; if she is feral or is allowed access to the outdoors she will bring back dead prey for them to investigate, recognize, and taste.

As the weeks go by and the kittens gain more control over their movements and skills, she brings back progressively less injured and more lively prey, so that the kittens can practice chasing and catching. But while chase and capture is a natural built-in behavior, killing is not entirely so—it must be learned and practiced. It is interesting to note that the nape or killing bite is not a behavior that is practiced in play, since this would be too dangerous a maneuver to try out on a sibling!

In a feral environment kittens have to be ready to go it alone by the time they are five months old. Their mother is likely to be in season again (if not already pregnant) and preparing to deal with the next litter. The kittens may be chased off to find their own territories.

learning to be sociable

Between three and thirteen weeks of age the kittens are in what is known as the socialization period—a time when they form relationships with their own species and practice different methods of communication. The period from two to eight weeks of age is a time when kittens can learn to interact with other species, too—if they miss out on these experiences at this early age it is unlikely they will ever be fully relaxed with individuals from other species. During this socialization period the kitten needs to be handled by lots of people so that it becomes relaxed around humans. This phase is critical to the making of a good pet—eight weeks seems to be a fairly clear cutoff point that makes all the difference between a feral cat and a pet, between wild and friendly. Occasionally, cats who meet people at this point remain nervous around everyone but their owner.

learning by observation

Kittens learn a great deal by observation. They have to implement many of their instinctive behaviors with practical lessons. For example, kittens naturally chase and catch anything that moves; however, they must learn which prey is dangerous (or even edible!) and need to learn how to kill it.

below: *Time to find out about all of the other creatures that are part of the family.*

left: *At three to four weeks old, kittens start to move from the nest to explore.*

below: *Safety in numbers—if things get scary, you can always huddle together!*

It has long been known that if you want a cat that is going to be a good hunter, choose a kitten from a queen with good hunting and killing skills—she will have taught her kittens well. Likewise, while kittens automatically scratch at loose soil or sand, observation of their mother using a litter box is enough for them to put the behavior and associations together and make them into the "clean" pets we love so much. Kittens learn to use a catflap in the door by observation, and scientists have found that under experimental conditions kittens that have been allowed to observe other cats undertaking a task are much quicker to pick it up than those that have not—they will be even quicker if they are allowed to watch the other cat learning the task in the first place.

There is no doubt that cats are intelligent creatures—it is not possible to measure this and compare it exactly with humans or other animals but cats show adaptability combined with a curiosity that makes them highly successful survivors and problem-solvers. Contrary to popular belief, they can be trained to undertake tasks—it is not as easy as with their canine cousins, but provided the motivations and rewards are appropriate, they can learn. However, cats will only do so if they want to—there is certainly no forcing them!

the look of the cat

Domestic cats (*Felis catus*) the world over look remarkably similar—even those breeds that developed initially in geographically isolated groups, such as the Siamese or Singapura, have different markings and slightly different body shapes but are amazingly similar in size and proportions. Even when man started to interfere and breed from certain cats to try to enhance or eliminate certain traits, the results made little difference. The beautiful semi-longhaired Maine Coon cat is said to be the largest breed and the Singapura the smallest; however, many cat breeds have individuals that span the size range. Compare this to dogs—for example the Great Dane and Chihuahua, whose size differential is huge.

It may be that the cat is somehow resistant to extreme modification or just that we have only been selectively breeding cats for about one hundred years compared to the thousands of years of selective breeding that have accompanied the man/dog relationship. Dogs have been bred for different work functions, and it is the function that has defined the size and shape of the dog—large to fight; small to fit down a rabbit or badger hole; lithe to run. We have never bred cats for work but merely for their looks, and this has made little impact on their basic "design," which

above: *Most people would agree that the feline form is pretty perfect as it is. As yet, man has only been able to change it a little.*

has been dictated by very specific predatory and dietary needs.

Resistance to change may also come about because the great majority of feline genes are responsible for the cat's exceptional physiology—only a small proportion deal with features such as shape or coat color, which is used to define breeds. It may also be that breeders have not yet unlocked the

secrets of breeding extreme sizes.
Many breeders do not want to
experiment with this, in case it results
in defects similar to those that blight
many of the canine breeds. Most
would agree that the feline form is just
about perfect as it is and that a cat
should be able to function as a cat,
maintaining its independence and
ability to take care of itself if necessary.

body shapes

The different breeds man has developed
or established can be defined by
referring to the cat's body shape and
proportions, the shape of the head, size,
and position of eyes and ears. At one
end of the range of forms are the
heavier stocky or cobby breeds, such as
the British shorthair or Persian, and at

the other are Oriental breeds such as the
Siamese, with slim bodies, fine limbs,
and a narrow wedge-shaped head.

coat variations

The coat colors and types we have
developed or selected are inherited
independently—that is, color varieties
can be found with every type of coat
and body shape. All cats are
fundamentally tabbies—the wild type
from which others have evolved.
Genetic changes can affect pigment

and how it is laid down in the hair.
A gene called the agouti gene is
responsible for the yellow/orange
banding on basically gray hair that is
also seen in other animals—the rabbit
is the best example of this—and the
coloration of the coat is excellent for
camouflage and merging into the
background. The pale banding on the
hairs in combination with tabby genes
gives rise to the various striped tabby
patterns with which we are familiar. In
cats with the non-agouti gene the

above left: *The curly and
sparse Rex-coated cats provide an
unusual variation in hair type.*

right: *The Munchkin has been
bred with short legs—the
majority of cat-lovers would find
this rather disturbing.*

above: *The Persian or Longhair has been developed with a long outer coat and thick undercoat.*

yellow bands are absent and replaced by darker colors to make a coat of uniform color—in fact the stripes are still there but color-matched. They can often be seen on the coats of young kittens—the tabby pattern looks like ghost markings.

The tabby coloring itself provides a pattern that breaks up a solid shape—the tiger's stripes and leopard's spots are good examples of coloring that is matched to the animal's environment.

left: *The Manx's coat is very thick and luxurious, though it does have a padded look.*

The African Wild Cat has agouti coloring and stripes, and these are probably the basis of the coloring we see in tabbies today. By experimenting with characteristics, breeders have developed the variety of coat colors and patterns we are familiar with.

siamese—color points

The Siamese is one of the most common breeds and one that most people instantly recognize—the genes involved reduce the pigment that colors the hair and eyes. There is more pigment at the extremes of the body—the amount of pigment present depends on temperature; the lower the temperature, the more pigment is produced. Similar coloring occurs in the Balinese, Birman, Tonkinese, and Himalayan breeds.

left: *The elegant Siamese has developed with color at its points (extremities), which are cooler than the rest of its body.*

right: *Tabby markings are part of the cat's camouflage in the wild, breaking up its solid shape.*

coat types

Hair length in pedigree cats is divided into short, long, and semi-long hair. There are also different coat types that are made up of combinations of the different hair types. A normal coat is made up of long guard hairs, awn hairs,

below: *All cats are tabbies underneath, but many have beautiful coat markings, including this Bengal. It's a pattern we have come to love and associate with people-friendly cats.*

and down or wool hairs. The guard hairs that form the top layer of the coat are covered with a scaly outer cuticle and a solid pigmented inside, and grow from individual follicles. The down hairs, known as secondary hairs, have air spaces between them, and are arranged like a ladder to make them soft. They are also usually fine and crinkled. Awn hairs are also secondary hairs that have thickened tips. Both down and awn

hairs grow in groups.

The shorthaired cat is the basic "wild" type but even this is only a generalization, and hair length varies considerably. Hair length is usually about 1.75 inches (4.5 cm) for the guard hairs. The Longhair or Persian has a very dense and long coat with a thick undercoat of down hairs that are almost as long as the guard hairs (as long as five inches [12.5 cm]). The hairs grow longer before they reach the rest or dormant phase of growth, resulting in a long and luxurious coat. In semi-longhairs and non-pedigree longhairs the undercoat is not so developed and so not as thick, and the guard hairs are long and silky.

above: *This Californian Spangled kitten will develop a muscular body, together with a coat that upon adulthood, closely resembles the king cheetah.*

The Cornish Rex has a soft, fairly sparse wavy coat that is characterized by a lack of guard hairs (caused by a genetic mutation). The wave is caused by the natural curl of the awn and down hairs, which do not grow to normal length. The American Wirehair breed has a much coarser coat that is also crimped and springy—in fact even the guard hairs are wavy or can be coiled into spirals. The "hairless" Sphynx actually has a thin covering of down over its skin.

While these coat color and body shape types contribute to the differences between the cats we are familiar with, they do not alter the fundamental nature of the cat (the solitary hunter, the champion sleeper, the adaptive survivor, the obligate carnivore). The cat has so far resisted any attempt to change its looks and character—we can only hope that humans do not push for change for the sake of it, for novelty or acclaim, and alter the fundamental cat present in all breeds.

right: *The cobby body shape and heavy bone structure of this blue British Shorthair make it a very attractive cat.*

right: *The Sphynx has very little hair; its fine, downy covering makes it appear "naked."*

eyes

The beauty of the cat lies not only in its shape, movement, and coat, but in those large and colorful eyes that have an iris that can range from yellow or orange through green to bright blue. Again the Siamese cat has clear blue eyes which differ from the blue-pigmented eyes of non-Siamese cats, and are the result of less pigment.

owning a **cat**

Owning a cat and living
with it in harmony is easier
if you understand feline
needs, both physical and
mental.

left: *Cats and people can have a very strong relationship that can last for 14 years or more.*

choosing your cat

Take good care of your cat, and, barring accidents and nonpreventable disease, it will live an average of 14 years and perhaps even into its 20s. Taking on a cat is a long-term partnership and one that grows more precious with time. And while many cats simply turn up and "adopt" their owners, if you do set out to choose a cat it is worth taking a little time to consider the type, sex, and temperament of cat that will best suit your circumstances and its needs.

Taking on a cat can be as easy and inexpensive as opening your back door and feeding the stray outside or, if you choose a breed that is still fairly new and in demand, it could cost hundreds of dollars. However, unlike different breeds of dog, which have very different personalities because they have been bred for certain tasks, cats, whatever they look like, all behave much the

left: *It's easy to love a small kitten, but the human/cat relationship also improves with time into a ripe and relaxed bond.*

same way. They have distinct personalities but these may differ as much within a breed as between them generally. So don't expect money to buy you anything much different than a non-pedigree cat—it may have a special coat color or length but underneath it all it is still basically an African Wild Cat. Of course there are breed tendencies and you can try to choose different characteristics, but whatever breed you choose, whether it is random or very selective, all cats' needs are very similar.

The joy of owning a cat is that almost anyone can keep one—they are much easier to live with than dogs. They don't need walks, they aren't dangerous to other people, and you can leave them during the day without worrying that they will chew up the furniture or soil your home. In fact they can be so easy to keep that we can forget that they are still independent animals with individual personalities that may not be quite as malleable as we would like.

Whatever we do we must not forget to respect the spirit of the cat and understand its basic needs. When this occurs the cat may exhibit a range of behaviors that can be at odds with what we expect from our felines— these are outlined on pages 92–103, but most are caused by expecting a cat to try to cope with an environment or with companions with which it cannot live contentedly.

right: *Building up the bond between you and your cats can be an entirely pleasurable experience for everyone.*

Consider the time you will have for a new cat, both initially and as time goes by. It is worth trying to spend a few days at home when you have a new cat or kitten to help it settle in and bond with you. Christmas and other occasions when the routine of the household is upset are not good times to get a new pet. Choose a quiet, calm time when the house is not full of strangers, or children who can get excited and unruly. Choose a time when you can give the new kitten some attention and when it can have quiet periods to sleep, to eat, and to learn about the layout of the house without distraction.

Are you out working for most of the day? If so it may be worth considering getting two kittens together to keep each other company and relieve you of the guilt of leaving one little ball of fur home alone when you go out. Of course this means twice the expense—particularly relevant if you choose two pedigree kittens—but it is much easier to introduce two kittens initially than to add one to a house where there is already a resident cat.

While most cats don't require a great deal of time on a regular basis (they love lots of attention but this can be when it suits cat and owner), if you imagine owning a longhaired Persian and visualize sitting with it on your lap, its flowing coat soft and beautiful, you must realize that the coat takes a lot of care and needs to be tended every day. The fully longhaired cat needs help to keep its coat tangle-free—it cannot be left to take care of itself.

Burmese and Siamese/Orientals have a reputation for being a bit more demanding than other breeds, and to an extent this is true—they enjoy human company and like to be involved in the everyday activities of the home. Being people-oriented and full of energy and inquisitiveness they may need more attention and care, so if you don't have time to give that and prefer a cat that will live alongside you without being demanding of your time, you may want to consider a different breed.

If you have never had a kitten or it is some time since you took on one of these small bundles of energy and mischief, you will be surprised how much time they do demand and what they can get into. They may well climb the curtains when they are a couple of months old and do circuits of the dining room halfway up the wall; if you have valuable knick-knacks, it is worth putting them away for at least six months. Cats grow up quickly and the craziness does eventually pass, but if all of this sounds a little trying for you perhaps you should consider taking on an older cat—there are thousands of such cats needing new homes, usually through no fault of their own.

While many dogs are put into shelters because they have behaviors their owners cannot live with, cats seldom have such problems and most adapt very well to new homes. By asking the right questions and trying to assess the cat yourself, you stand a good chance of taking on a loving cat that has passed the crazy kitten years and would be delighted to join you in the comfort of your home and give you love and companionship feline-style.

If you live in an urban area or one that would be extremely dangerous for a free-roaming cat, it is possible to keep a cat totally indoors or provide it with a fenced-in run in the yard. Keeping a cat indoors should not be undertaken lightly—it suits some cats and not others, and can lead to frustration and behavior problems. If you are considering having an indoor cat, you need to get a kitten that has not been outside, or preferably two kittens together who can keep each other company while you are out, neither of which has seen much of the outside world—the theory is "what you haven't had you won't miss." This works for some cats but it becomes obvious that others still have a great drive to get outdoors—it will probably become noticeable as the cat develops.

Some tips for improving the "amusement value" of your home include building more vertical structures—shelves and perches—for cats to exercise on, which give them an opportunity to "escape" from the usual areas. Rather than have lots of toys available all the time, select a few and change them regularly so that the novelty value is not lost; provide a viewing shelf by the window so the cat can be amused by the goings-on outdoors (unless this causes frustration because the cat wants to go out); hide food for the cat to find (this is called "environmental enrichment" in zoos); play chase and hunt games with your cat; provide lots of new "toys" such as cardboard boxes and paper tunnels.

Do not attempt to keep a cat indoors if it has previously had a free lifestyle. The only exceptions to this would be the very nervous cat that would choose to stay indoors even if given the freedom to go out, or an older cat that is happy to stay in and has given up its hunting and wandering habits in exchange for warmth and security.

If you already have a cat or dog the introduction of a new cat can be difficult. If your resident cat is already

neutered and you plan to neuter the new one, the sex of the newcomer will probably not matter. However, it can be useful to choose a cat of the opposite sex just to cut down on any possible turmoil. Kittens present less of a territorial threat to a resident cat and are less likely to become aggressive themselves so you will only have to deal with the repercussions of putting the resident cat's monopoly on your affection in question. If you are taking on another adult cat then it is probably wise to choose one of the

left: *Many animal welfare societies care for cats while they work hard to find homes for them.*

opposite sex, and make your introductions carefully. It may take quite some time for the cats to even tolerate each other but be patient and calm and it may work.

If you are about to start a family yourself it is probably wise to wait until your baby is a few months old before you get a kitten. In this way you can get over the initial traumas new babies inevitably bring and get back into a household routine before the kitten arrives. A new kitten coming in will take this as normal because it will not have become used to a childless house. Cats and children mix quite happily as long as you take the obvious hygiene and safety precautions and teach the children from a very early age to respect the cat.

Having to be away from home several times a year can discourage people from getting a cat because they worry about it when they are away. This can be overcome by finding a high quality cattery where your cat will be cared for to the highest standards.

choosing a kitten

A cat should be yours for life—that can mean 14 or more years, so it is important to choose one not only for its looks but also for personality. All too often we make a choice of a kitten purely on the color or markings on its coat, and while a great deal of

above: *Cats and children can have an excellent relationship, as long as the children are taught how to behave with the cat.*

the pleasure we obtain from our feline companions is derived from their looks and graceful feline form, personality is extremely important, too. The great majority of cats make excellent pets but sometimes early experiences from kittenhood mean that they will never make confident and rewarding pets.

Kittens should also be fully vaccinated or at least have had their first vaccination before they go to their new homes. There are many excellent

breeders but there are also some who are inexperienced or uninformed and are not aware of the importance of socializing kittens in their very early weeks.

On pages 52–57 the development of kittens is outlined and the importance of their first weeks explained. Before they reach eight weeks old kittens need to meet and experience a wide range of different people, other animals, new noises, and objects. They will then be able to approach life confidently. Thus, when going to see kittens, it is vital to find out how they were kept in these early weeks. If they grew up in a shed or building away from the household environment and its everyday routines, they may not be able to deal with life confidently. Of course hygiene and disease control are

important but experience of life at an early age is equally vital for a happy pet cat to develop.

Likewise, if you are choosing a non-pedigree kitten from a family home, see how it has been reared. The difference here is that you may be able to take the kitten home from as early as six weeks—the average age is usually about seven or eight weeks, provided it has been weaned (which it should be by this time). Thus you have a chance to let it experience your home while it is still at a stage when it is open to absorbing new experiences that will affect its future personality.

Of course, you will probably have a preference for coat color or pattern— some people love gingers, some like good old black and white kittens, or, if you have chosen a pedigree cat, there are subtle differences between kittens even in those breeds where there is only one color. However, personality is important, and even though cats do

change as they grow and there is no guarantee that you will choose the perfect pet cat, you can avoid obvious problems.

When you go to see the litter it is extremely tempting to want to bring home a kitten no matter what it is like. If you are choosing a pedigree kitten you will probably visit first and choose your kitten, and have to wait until it is old enough to be moved to a new home. However, the same tips apply—don't choose one if you are not happy with it. Most people want a cat that is happy to join in with the family, will be confident with people it knows and willing to meet visitors, will be able to deal with the normal household activities, and will go in and out without fuss.

Talk to the owners of the kittens before you visit. If you have a dog or children, try to choose kittens from the same type of background—if they have been used to dogs from a very early

interested in climbing around or playing, but as long as it does not run away or try to hide from you it should be able to deal with life. If it looks ill, avoid it—once you get the kitten into your home everyone will fall in love with it and illness or death is going to be very traumatic for everyone concerned, and it may also cost you a lot of money in veterinary fees. In fact, if any of the kittens looks ill, avoid the whole litter—if one is infected with a disease, it is probable that the others will be, too.

Avoid the poor little kitten that is cowering under the furniture or at the back of a box—you may feel sorry for it but evidence suggests that if a kitten is nervous and it is more than eight weeks old, it is likely to remain nervous. Of course there are exceptions, but if you want a confident outgoing cat, this is much more likely if it already has this type of personality when young.

If you are offered a feral kitten—one that has been born to a cat that has had little or no association with people but has been trapped or rescued as part of a neutering program,

age they will think they are a normal part of life. Likewise, if they have been handled by children and are used to the high-pitched screaming or laughing they will not be alarmed when they meet your children for the first time. Ask if they have grown up in the home or in a shed at the back of the yard, and how much interaction they have had with people.

Watch all the kittens and interact with them. See how confident their mother is and how she interacts with her owners. Obviously she will be affected by having new people in the house when her kittens are there, but if she is relatively happy with people around she is likely to have conveyed this to her kittens.

Choose a kitten that looks healthy and is happy to be picked up and stroked. It will probably be more

right: *A confident cat will enjoy joining in with everyday activities in the home and garden.*

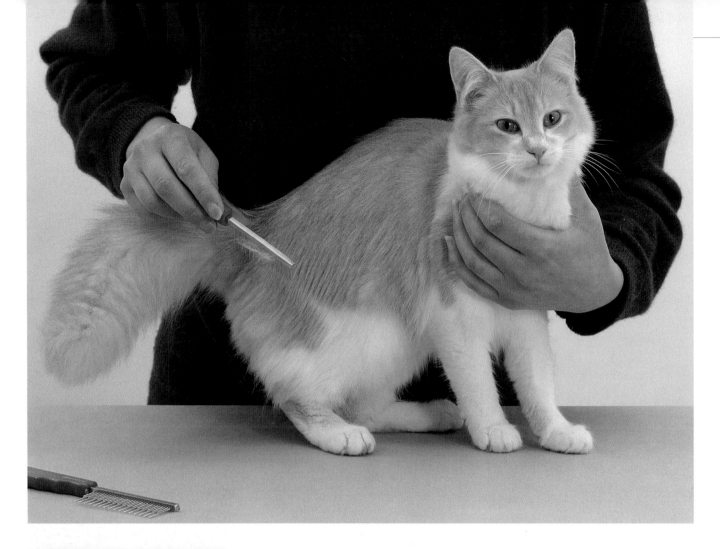

or found in someone's yard—think about it very carefully. If you can get hold of such a kitten early enough, you should be able to give it positive experiences before it reaches the critical eight weeks old, and it will develop as a normal pet cat. There is such a thin line between pet and wild cat, and this can make the difference between a rewarding or very distant "pet."

If you are taking on an adult cat you will probably get it from an animal shelter. Again there are some points to look out for. Most of the cats will be there through no fault of their own,

but it is worth trying to find out something about their backgrounds. You may be able to find out if a cat is used to children or dogs, or should not be kept with either. A cat may be there because it has not settled into a multi-cat household, and so should be avoided if you already have a cat.

Again, go into the cat's pen and see how it interacts with you. Ask the

sexing your kitten: *If you buy a kitten from a breeder, you can rely on his or her expertise to tell you what sex it is (it can be difficult to sex very young kittens but it becomes easier as they grow). However, if the kitten's owners are inexperienced you may want to double-check.*

above left: *A female cat—the openings are close together and look like the letter "i."*

left: *A male cat—there are small testicles under the anus, and the penis is below these.*

left: *left: A cat with longer hair needs to be brushed regularly, and therefore requires more of the owner's time and care.*

people who run the shelter what type of personality the cat has and any tips they can give you. They will want to try and match you to one that suits you so that it can be provided with a stable and loving home.

One of the most vital factors in choosing a cat from a shelter is health. In general avoid shelters where cats are kept in large groups—for example houses with tens or even hundreds of cats kept together or just grouped separately in different rooms. This is a hotbed for infection. Many such cats will not have been vaccinated and may be carrying cat flu, leukemia, or immunodeficiency virus. Many viruses can remain dormant within the body until the cat becomes stressed—and

what could be more stressful for a primarily solitary animal than being crammed in with a huge number of other cats in a strange environment, with nowhere to escape to? Little wonder that some types of "rescue" often create more damage than they fix.

However, a well-run animal shelter where cats are kept in clean accommodations, either individually or in small groups once they have gone through a quarantine period, will understand the problems of infection and take as many precautions as possible to keep and reacclimate healthy cats. They may also have vaccinated and neutered the cats, and tested them for various infectious diseases.

below: *If you choose a nervous cat, you may find it difficult to coax it into its new environment and make it part of your family.*

Checklist for health

- Wherever you get your cat or kitten, find out if and when it was vaccinated, wormed, or tested for any diseases. Ask for a vaccination certificate if there is one.
- Follow your instincts—if you feel something is not quite right, say so. You could take your kitten for a full check-up once you have gotten it. If problems are noticed, you have the chance to decide whether you want to treat it or take it back before you become too attached to it.
- Look at the eyes, ears, mouth, and nose. There should be no discharge or obvious injuries. The eyes should be bright and the third eyelid (it looks like a white membrane over the lower part of the eye) should not be visible.
- The coat should be glossy, with no bare patches or flaky skin.
- Ears should be clean and healthy-looking. Deposits of wax may mean that the cat is suffering from ear mites.
- Gums should be pink and healthy. Teeth should be white and the breath should not smell. If you are taking on an older cat it is probable that its teeth will need some care—this is something to check with your vet when you get home.
- The cat or kitten should not be snuffling or sneezing and its breathing should not be noisy or wheezy.
- Look under the cat's tail—it should look clean and healthy and there should be no signs of diarrhea such as soiled fur or reddening of the skin.
- The cat or kitten should walk without stumbling or limping and without pain.

your **new** cat
the first **24 hours**

Bringing home a new cat or kitten can be traumatic for everyone—owners as well as felines! Owners want to make their new charge feel as relaxed as possible, and to be able to reassure the cat that everything will be fine.

For any cat or kitten a change of environment is a stressful time. For a kitten it will be the first time it has been in a car, the first time away from its mother, and the first time it has been out of the house it was born in. So while it could be a very traumatic time, kittens are very resilient and are at a time of life when they are still adaptable; their curiosity and energy usually get the better of them and they soon gain confidence. The kittens that deal with change best are those that have already had early lives full of interest and novelty. They have learned to deal with new situations and will soon take the changes in their stride. Kittens that have only met one or two people and have not been taken out of the place where they were born may find it harder to adapt.

left: *You need to provide a litter box for your new cat, even if you eventually want it to go outdoors.*

right: *A pen or cage is an ideal way to introduce a new cat or kitten to a household that already has pets.*

An adult cat may find adapting even more difficult than a kitten and, being much more aware of danger, will probably take some time to relax. However, there are things that are important to cats that you can do to help them feel at home.

traveling home

Tempting as it may be to cuddle your new cat or kitten on the way home, it is wiser to put it in a secure carrier and either place it behind the front seat or strap the carrier onto the seat with the seatbelt so that it does not move around. If you are driving and don't have a passenger to take care of the kitten it must go in a carrier for your safety and its own. Kittens can be very lively in the car or crawl under seats if they are frightened. Adult cats can be unpredictable, especially if you

do not know how they will react in new situations. They may also urinate or defecate in the car, so it may be best to confine them to a washable basket.

Do not use a disposable cardboard carrier—the determined cat will be able to claw its way out, and if it does urinate the cardboard will become soggy and disintegrate. Covering the carrier with a blanket or sheet may make the cat feel more secure for the journey. If you are traveling a long distance and the cat must be in the car for three or four hours you need to give it access to a litter box and a drink of water at some point.

Quite often cats are vocal in the car and meow pitifully all the way home—while they make a great deal

left: *Initial introductions can be made safer and less traumatic by using a cage.*

of noise, they are not coming to any harm, and it is usually the owner who needs the Valium to deal with the noise!

security

Security is very important to cats—they need to feel that the space they live in is their territory and safe from invaders. When you take your new cat or kitten home, make it comfortable in one warm room.

Provide a cozy bed—it may be useful to use your cat carrier as a bed so that the cat can hide in it until it feels a little more confident. If you have a puppy crate or kittening pen—a pen about 3 x 2 x 2 feet (90 x 60 x 60 cm)—this can be a very useful "den" for a new kitten. Put in it a warm dry bed (even a cardboard box

with blankets will do) and give it a litter box. The kitten can be put into the pen for a rest, or when you go out and want to be sure it will stay out of trouble. It can also be used for introduction to other animals in the household (see pages 85–87). If the cat came in a bed or with a blanket, don't replace it with a clean one but leave the one it is familiar with, for a few days at least. This will help it to make the transition.

smelling at home

Never underestimate the power of smell for the cat. Not only will your home look strange to the cat, but it will also smell very alien, with nothing familiar to help the cat feel secure.

You can help it by doing something very simple. Take a cotton cloth or handkerchief and gently rub it over the cat, concentrating on its face, under its chin, and around its temples. This is where the scent glands it uses to mark

its home are situated. Dab the cloth around the room, on the furniture, and even on yourself. The cat will recognize the scent and will feel much more secure—it is like bringing your own furniture and clothes with you to make yourself feel at home somewhere new.

patience

Your new cat may not use the bed you provide or come to you for comfort initially, preferring to hide under the couch and peep out when all is quiet, but take things slowly and quietly. Do not chase the cat or kitten. Speak quietly, coax with warmth, attention, and food, and wait for the cat to get its bearings. Give it time to calm down and give it space to do so.

You may feel like sitting and cuddling it to provide comfort but it may want to sit on its own and come to you when it is ready to. Likewise, when you introduce your resident cats or dogs (see page 85) to the newcomer, do not expect instant results—it can take months before they get along well.

If you have taken on a young kitten remember that, like a young child, it will need to sleep quite a lot and should be given space and time away from adults and children who want to hold it and play with it.

above: *Provide a snug, draft-free bed for your new cats to rest and sleep in.*

left: *Two's company—twice the trouble but lots of fun! It is easier to get two kittens together than to introduce another cat later on.*

litter training

Whether you bring home a new kitten or an adult cat you will need to supply a litter box, even if it is only for a few weeks, before the cat goes outdoors. You may have a strong preference for a certain type of litter because it is easier to use, or lighter to carry, or makes less mess. There are many types of litter on the market, the most common being clay-based, pelleted sawdust or paper, and fine-grain litter. However, initially,

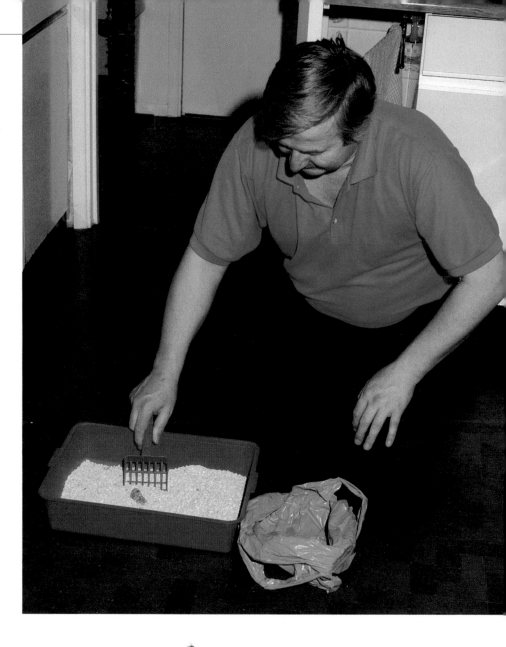

left: *Litter boxes need to be cleaned regularly to keep them from smelling, and cats will not use a box that is too dirty.*

it is best to stick to the same litter as the cat/kitten has been used to, so that there is some continuity and not everything it has to deal with is totally new. You can then gradually mix some of the litter you prefer into it so that the changeover is not abrupt.

When cats urinate or defecate they dig a hole, use it, then cover it up, scratching the soil over the top. They need to be able to carry out this most natural of behaviors in the box—thus it must be big enough and deep enough to hold enough litter to do this. Even if you do not put litter in the box you will see the cat carry out "digging and covering" actions with its paws, digging imaginary soil and trying to cover up the urine or feces again.

Some litters have added air fresheners or scents to mask the smell of soiled litter in the box, but if these smell strong to us they are probably even more overpowering to cats—if bad odors from a box are a problem it would be better just to clean out the box a little more frequently. Some people use newspaper in the litter box, but there are dangers to this: Ink may come off the paper onto the cat's feet and be carried

left: *A box needs to be deep enough to prevent litter from being kicked over the side.*

right: *Provide the playful cat—especially younger ones—with a selection of toys.*

around the house, or it may be toxic if licked—the cat may also come to associate all newspapers with depositing waste!

Positioning of the litter box is important, too. Cats do not like to defecate near where they eat; thus while it may seem logical to place the box, food, and bed all together in the

above: *Kittens are usually litter-trained by their mother—they only need to be shown where the tray is and they soon get the idea.*

"cat's corner," the cat will probably prefer to eat away from the box. Squatting is also a fairly vulnerable position for a cat, especially a nervous

Kittens take an interest in food from about a month old. They are usually fully weaned and on solid food by seven or eight weeks.

scent reminder to help the kitten make the association. Never punish the kitten for getting it wrong—this will make it frightened and more likely to choose a hidden spot as a toilet— simply place it in the box and praise it when it gets it right.

introducing children

Introductions to other cats or dogs in the family are probably better left until at least the day after you have arrived home with your new cat or kitten—it will have enough to contend with just getting a grip on its new environment. However, if you have children it is very difficult to keep them away for more than about five minutes when you get home—they will be very excited about meeting a new pet, and are likely to rush in with great enthusiasm and a lot

one. So if you have a box placed in an open part of the house or a walkway that is used by dogs, cats, and children, the cat may be very reluctant to use it.

Choose a spot that is quiet and feels secure—in a corner, behind some furniture, or in an open closet. Buying a tray that has a lid or making a cover, using a cardboard box with a hole cut in it for access, will also make the cat feel more secure—it only has to worry about danger coming from one direction. A covered tray is also neater because enthusiastic digging does not result in litter spilling over the edge and all over the floor. It is also useful for cats with a bad aim! Make sure it cannot be used as a sandbox by toddlers or a snackbar by the dog,

litter training your kitten

Litter training kittens is much easier than housebreaking puppies, but this should not come as a surprise—the training has almost always already been done by the mother cat. We merely have to show the kitten where the box is and remind it to go there after feeding.

By watching the queen and following their natural instincts to rake soil-type substrates, kittens soon associate toileting behavior and the litter box. You can help to remind your kitten by placing it in the box and raking its paws through the litter—it will soon get the idea again.

Put it in the box regularly, especially after it has eaten or woken up. Clean up any "accidents" with tissue or a cloth, and place this in the box as a

above: *Cat food varies from dry to semi-moist to wet (canned) types.*

of noise. This can be somewhat alarming for a new feline resident. Explain how frightening an experience like this could be for the cat and how they can make it feel welcome by being quiet and gentle.

If the cat or kitten has come from a household with children it will probably take it all in its stride, but if it has not you need to go slowly and avoid sudden movements or loud noises. Sit the children on the floor and let the cat or kitten approach them. Show them how to stroke the cat on its back where it is likely to enjoy being touched, and avoid picking it up or squeezing it. Short, quiet meetings are best so that children do not get overexcited and the new cat or kitten is not overwhelmed by attention. After a few days the excitement usually dies down as the novelty wears off.

feeding

Moving to a new home can be stressful and cause stomach upsets in cats and kittens. Therefore it is wise not to change the cat's diet immediately but to continue with the diet it was eating before the move. This gives your new pet time to settle a little before its digestive system has to take on a new food. When it has settled in you can decide what you want to feed it.

Do not overfeed the newcomer—it can be very tempting to offer it comfort and affection by giving lots of food, but this can overload the digestive system and result in diarrhea. Offer small amounts regularly—kittens need to eat more often than cats—to give it time to digest the food. Only offer milk if the cat is used to it. Some cats cannot digest cows' milk and this can cause sickness or diarrhea too, so clean water is sufficient.

below: *A wide range of bowls is available to suit all preferences. There are also feeders that open at preset times if you need to go out at your cats' mealtimes.*

the first week

After the initial excitement of the first day, you can start to get to know your cat, train it to the ways of your house (as much as you can train a cat), and change the type of food and/or litter it has been accustomed to over to the types you want it to have.

staying indoors

You will need to keep an adult cat indoors for at least two weeks to help it bond to your home as its new territory. A new kitten needs to stay indoors, too, especially if it has not had its vaccinations. If you have bought a pedigree kitten from a reputable breeder it will have had at least one of its vaccinations before you get it, and will have some protection. Most

pedigree kittens will have completed their vaccination course and come to you protected against cat flu and feline panleukopenia. You will still need to

give the vaccine about ten days after the actual injection to reach its maximum protection for the cat. Non-pedigree kittens are not usually

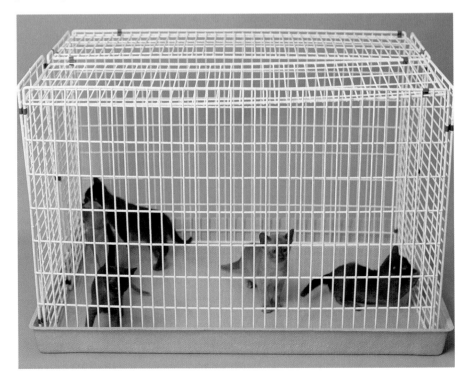

right: *A kittening pen can be an extremely useful tool for introductions and keeping your kitten safe while you are out.*

left: *After you have chosen your kitten you will need to provide warmth and comfort—it will feel strange, away from its mother and littermates.*

vaccinated before they go to their new homes at around seven or eight weeks. Therefore vaccination is a priority and can normally begin at eight weeks old.

If you have a resident cat, make sure it is up to date with its vaccinations—infections can be brought in by newcomers, as well as picked up from residents. If you have a number of cats it may be wise to keep the new kitten separated from them until it has had its vaccinations and has come through the changeover of homes. This is because stress—and leaving Mom and the only home you know can cause a great deal of stress—is often a trigger for disease.

Stress seems to decrease the kitten's ability to mount an immune response to infection, and makes it vulnerable to catching disease. It can also cause the kitten to "shed" a virus—this occurs when the cat or kitten is carrying a disease, and although it may not actually show many signs of disease, the virus is excreted via the feces and sometimes in the saliva.

Consequently, bringing new cats or kittens into your home can often be a trigger for disease. You can keep the possibility of infection to a minimum by making sure all cats are vaccinated, treated for worms and other parasites (see pages 110–112), and well fed, and that stress is kept to a minimum.

hygiene

Hygiene is also important—don't let the litter box become too dirty since this can be a main source of infection if cats are sharing. For this reason it is best to let the newcomer have its own litter box, initially at least.

To begin with you should clean out the box about every two days, removing the solids with a scoop as they appear.

In this way it will smell like a latrine and the cat will learn to associate the litter with its toileting area. However, if it becomes too soiled the cat or kitten will not want to use it.

Wash the box regularly with hot water and disinfect it weekly. Be careful in your choice of disinfectants—cats are particularly sensitive to certain chemicals found in disinfectants,

left: *Visit your vet as soon as possible if your kitten has not had its vaccinations.*

notably phenols. In general it is best to avoid disinfectants that turn cloudy white when they are put in water. Dilute the disinfectant as directed in the instructions—do not be tempted to use a higher strength solution, as this could increase toxicity. If you have a number of cats, provide a box for each cat and initially try to direct a new kitten to its own box to minimize any disease risks.

Keep food and water bowls clean, and again keep the new cat's bowls and any resident cats' bowls separate until vaccinations are finalized and cats have settled in. Some people prefer to keep pets' and humans' dishes separate; other

below: *Fresh water should always be available. Some cats prefer water directly from the tap.*

people will put them in the dishwasher with everything else each day.

Likewise, some people are very meticulous about not having cats on work surfaces and tables—if you don't want your cat or kitten to go on the surfaces, be consistent and gently remove it each time it jumps up. Don't leave tempting scraps of food on kitchen surfaces, since this encourages such behavior. If your cat just likes to sit on kitchen surfaces to gain enough height to be able to oversee the kitchen, provide some high vantage points and encourage the cat to sit there instead of on the food preparation surfaces.

feeding
Cats must eat meat (see pages 12–13) and are natural "snackers," eating lots

of small meals a day as they would if they were catching ten or more mice a day to survive. You can feed your cat in a variety of different ways, depending on the cat's preferences and your lifestyle.

If you are at home all day you can actively give lots of small meals and use them to build bonds with your cat— feeding time is a great time for interaction and training (usually the cat training the owner that a meow means "feed me please"). If you are out for most of the day you may feed less frequent large meals or leave out a nutritional dry cat food that the cat can nibble all day.

Cats fed on moist food (canned or foil-wrapped food) tend to eat bigger meals, perhaps because flavor, taste, and smell are at their most potent when

the can or packet is freshly opened. However, canned food is more likely to go bad if left uneaten. Canned food will probably provide your cat with all the water it needs, but always have a bowl of clean water available—this is especially important if you feed a dry diet exclusively.

Kittens especially need to be fed small meals throughout the day (about five times a day for an 8- to 12-week-old kitten), since they have small stomachs but large needs in terms of energy for growth—small frequent meals allow them to ingest and digest enough nutrients to grow rapidly. Growing kittens gain about a third of an ounce (10 g) of body weight per day from birth to five or six months of age, so the diet needs to provide all the kitten requires nutritionally, as well as the extra demands of coping with the stresses of a new home and any infections.

Pet food manufacturers produce food that is specially tailored for kittens, to provide energy and extra vitamins and minerals—they can be fed this for the first six months or so of life.

Choose a good quality diet your cat seems to enjoy and that does not result in diarrhea. You can feed your own homemade diet but it can be very difficult to get the balance of nutrients and energy right, and it can be time-consuming. When your new kitten has settled in you can gradually mix the diet of your choice into its original diet in increasing quantities so that the changeover is staggered and not a shock to the kitten's system.

Feed your cat or kitten in a quiet spot well away from other animals that may compete for food, and where it can concentrate on the food without interruption.

Be careful about automatically giving your new pet milk—when kittens become weaned they lose the ability to digest lactose, a sugar that is found in milk, and can suffer from stomach

upset if they are allowed to drink it.

introductions to resident cats

Even though your reason for getting another cat or kitten may be to keep your resident cat company, it may not rush out and welcome the newcomer with open paws! Indeed, as outlined on pages 30–31, cats do not necessarily want to be sociable, and they don't need to be for survival in the wild. There is no need for them to accept the new arrival as part of the group, and it is of no benefit to them to do so.

However, if cats are kept together from kittenhood, or if they are given time to get used to each other and there is no shortage of food, sleeping places, or space, they can and do get along. Cats are great individualists—some enjoy companionship, while others merely tolerate company and live parallel lives under the same roof. Some cannot tolerate another feline in the same home at all.

How you introduce a new cat or kitten into your home and to a resident cat or cats can make the difference between success or failure. If a relationship becomes violent or fearful it can be very difficult to reverse the reactions that the cat feels are vital to its survival; so careful introductions that prevent excessive trauma are important.

Remember that scent is the most important of the cat's senses in terms of communication and social well-being. You can try to integrate the new cat into your home and make it feel less alien by transferring some "smells of home" onto it before you introduce it to the resident cat. Likewise, letting the cat get used to the new smells of the house and the scents of other pets makes initial meetings less traumatic. For this reason it can be very useful to postpone the meeting of the cats for a few days or even a week, and during this time keep them in

above: *The cat is a natural "snacker," as it would be in the wild, hunting countless mice to maintain its diet.*

separate rooms. Then switch them over, allowing each to investigate the other's room and rest area. Additionally you can stroke each cat and mix scents in this way; you can also gather scent from around the head area and dab it on the other cat. It will take time for the resident cat to realize that the new cat is not a threat and for the new cat to accept the presence of the old one.

It is up to you to make both the new cat and the resident feel as secure as possible and prevent the newcomer from being chased or threatened. The best way to do this is to use a kittening pen, indoor crate, or a cat basket for initial introductions. This allows the cats to see each other, sniff through the bars, and hiss and grumble at each other without any attack or intimidation.

Make the new cat or kitten comfortable in the carrier or pen. If you have taken on a new kitten a kittening pen or dog crate—a metal mesh pen with a door that can be left open or securely shut if you want to keep the kitten in—is ideal as its "den." You can put its bed and litter box inside and use it as a base for the kitten. Introductions can be made using the pen and you can shut the kitten in if you are going out and don't want to leave it where it can get into mischief or into danger. The kitten can be shut in the pen at night for safety and still integrate with any animals kept in the room. If you can't get hold of a pen or crate, you can use a cat carrier for actual introductions. Of course, you won't be able to shut the cat or kitten in it for long periods, because it is too small, but it can be very useful.

If you are using a crate, place the cat or kitten in it and let the resident cat come into the room. If you are using a cat carrier, place it above ground level so the cats are not forced into direct eye contact with each other—this can be an aggressive act between cats. Let the resident cat into the room and give it attention and calm reassurance. If the cat decides to run away, let it go and try again later—these things may take a little time. If the cats show signs of aggression, distract them with a noise and praise them for quiet encounters.

Feed both cats in the same room with a special treat and gradually move the resident cat's bowl nearer to the cage so that they are sharing space and relaxing together to eat. Place the crate carrier on the floor and feed again close together. Throughout the process, and especially initially, there may be some hissing and spitting but this should calm down into curiosity and gradually acceptance.

There is no set time for all these procedures—it may only take a day or two, or it may take several weeks. It may even take months before the cats are fully relaxed with each other, but if you can reach the stage of a calm truce between them you are well on the way to success!

Problems can arise if initial meetings are allowed to end in a chase or a fight, and where either cat is very frightened by the other. This can take a long time to overcome (if ever), and is why the crate or carrier system works so well in keeping the situation under control. When you decide the time is right to let them meet without the pen, use a favorite food to distract them and feed them some distance apart. Make sure that there is somewhere for the new cat to run and hide if it feels the need, and be ready to interrupt if the situation gets nasty.

After the new cat or kitten has met the resident cat and become comfortable with its own room then it can be allowed to investigate the rest of the house slowly, room by room.

introducing the dog

If your dog is already used to cats in the house he will know that felines rule the roost, and how to act around them. Likewise, if the new cat or kitten

left: *There is a wide array of grooming brushes and combs available from pet stores and at cat shows.*

below left: *Get your kitten used to being groomed from an early age, and it will become part of normal life.*

below: *Even shorthaired cats will enjoy being groomed and learn to sit still while it is being done.*

is from a household that had a dog it may react cautiously at first but will not be unduly alarmed, and will relax fully once they have met and become familiar with each other. If you have not had a cat before you will need to keep things under control until the cat and dog have gotten used to each other. Once again the use of a carrier or pen is ideal to keep the situation calm and let the dog sniff the cat through the cage.

Young pups are likely to get very excited and may try to "play" with the newcomer, who is unlikely to want to join in. Breeds such as terriers or greyhounds may need to be kept under strict control until they have accepted the cat as part of the family and not as "fair game." Be careful that a sudden movement from the cat does not induce a chase. Praise the dog for calm interactions and progress to using a leash for introductions outside the pen when you feel the time is right. Use food and treats to encourage and reward the dog.

left: *Keep dogs under strict control for initial introductions, so that chases do not result. Be calm and reassuring.*

grooming

For shorthaired cats or kittens grooming help from humans is not essential—it may be something you want to do, or the cat may enjoy the attention, but it is not vital to its well-being. However, if you have taken on a longhaired cat such as a Persian you will need to groom it regularly, if not daily, to prevent its thick coat from becoming tangled and matted.

The best way to make grooming fun is to start as early as possible in kittenhood when the coat is shorter and when the kitten can learn that it is a pleasant interaction with its owner and a normal part of the daily routine. Start with short sessions (a couple of minutes) and be very gentle and encouraging, making it enjoyable for the kitten and yourself.

If you have taken on a longhaired adult cat, see how it is settling in and how it reacts to grooming in its first week. If it is still very unsettled or reacts violently to being approached by brush and comb, take things slowly and carefully, again with brief attempts to groom. If you feel the cat needs more time to settle, don't rush things.

the first six months

After the excitement of getting your new kitten or cat, finding out about its character, changing it over to the food and litter you want to use, ensuring it has had all its vaccinations, is wormed and treated for fleas (see pages 110–112), you are ready to consider letting it out in the big wide world. Although some people keep their cats permanently indoors because of busy roads or other dangers, most cat owners let their cats go out to carve a niche for themselves in the great outdoors, and there's do doubt that most cats love going outside and putting their hunting and survival skills into practice.

below: *Talk to your vet about the right time to neuter your kitten. It is usually done when the cat is between four and six months old.*

first time out

If your new cat or kitten wasn't vaccinated when you got it, you need to keep it in for about ten days after it has had its final vaccination or booster so that its immune system has time to build its defenses. Cats need about two weeks indoors in a new home to help them bond to it before you let them go out.

When the time comes to let it out, plan to take the cat out for a walk around the yard. You want to be able to attract the cat's attention and coax it back in again fairly quickly, then repeat the operation a little while later so that the cat learns how to get back home.

It is useful to have worked out a signal with your cat that means it is going to be fed—you could bang its dish or can of food, or make a sound, or use a word that it associates with being fed. It should then rush excitedly to the kitchen. It will not take long to do this simple bit of training, and it gives you a signal that the cat knows and understands, and that makes it eager to come back into the house with you. You can heighten its enthusiasm for food by not feeding it for a while before this. Each time you go out let the cat explore a little more before you call it in, so that it learns the route home gradually.

using a catflap

Most adult cats know how to use a catflap, but if your new cat doesn't, train it in the same way you would a new kitten. First of all, simply prop the flap open with a stick, tie it up with a

above: *A catflap set in a door is a convenient and secure way of allowing your pet to come and go whenever it wants to, whether you are in or out. Make sure there is a locking system on the catflap you buy, so that you have the option of keeping your cats in and other people's out.*

box closer to the door, to the outside, or to the catflap.

Dig up a piece of ground so that it is soft and easy to use—cats automatically dig in soft, freshly dug soil and kittens love to play at this when they first discover the soil. If it is solid and difficult to dig they will not be tempted to use it. If you spread some of the soiled litter onto this initially, it also helps the cat to associate the soil with a litter site. Cover any children's sandboxes, as these will be seen as ideal large litter boxes.

piece of string, or tape it open. Coax the cat in and out using food or a game, such as pulling a toy through the hole. Use lots of praise, never lose your temper or frighten the cat, and make it fun to use.

Once the cat has gotten the idea of climbing through the hole, prop the flap about halfway open so that the cat has to push it slightly on the way out or in. Gradually prop it open less and less, then remove the prop altogether so the cat has to push it open itself.

Make sure the flap is not too stiff for a small kitten or a cat that is unsure of itself to use. It will quickly get the idea—in fact if you have a resident cat that regularly uses the flap, a new kitten can learn just by watching and copying; you may not even have to teach it at all.

removing the litter box

If you want your cat or kitten to transfer from using a litter box to using the yard as a latrine, again, do it gradually and help the cat by mixing some soil with the litter. Move the

feeding

By six months old (when your kitten is about 75 percent grown), you can feed it two meals a day. If you are feeding dry food on a free-choice basis, obviously your cat or kitten will have decided how many meals it wants to have every day.

When your cat is fully grown—around one year old—start to monitor its weight; if it begins to put on fat, alter the amount of food you give. Most young cats are very active and excess weight is not a problem. It can be more of a cause for worry in indoor, older, or inactive cats. If you are worried about feeding, ask your veterinarian.

provide a scratch post

One of the cat's natural behaviors is stropping its claws—this not only keeps the claws sharp but is a marking behavior, too. Cats usually confine their scratching to the outdoors but some, probably for marking rather than sharpening reasons, scratch indoors. Of course, cats kept permanently indoors will have to find an outlet for this behavior.

Provide your cat with a scratch post—there are many types available, but try to choose one that allows the cat to stretch and pull down or across it, as it would when using a tree or post outdoors. Remember too that a carpet-covered post may signal that any carpet is available and acceptable as a scratching area—stairs are often a favorite.

identification

You may need your cat to wear a collar to enable it to carry a magnet or electronic key to a selective catflap, or you may want your cat to wear an identification tag on its collar in case it gets lost. Be sure to buy one that is elasticized, has a safety catch, or simply pulls over the cat's head, in case it gets caught on a branch or in case the cat gets a foot stuck through it. Secure it

fairly tightly so that it does not slip off—you should be able to put two fingers underneath it. A fluorescent or reflective collar also provides extra safety on roads in low light conditions.

You may also consider having your cat microchipped for permanent identification. A tiny device about the size of a grain of rice is implanted under the skin using a special needle, and the cat's identity is logged onto a national computer database. Should it become lost and be taken to an animal shelter, its identity can be read by a scanner and the owner contacted.

neutering

There is an old wives' tale that suggests it is best to let a cat have one litter before neutering—there is no sound reason for this and unless you wish to breed for specific reasons it is best to have your cat neutered.

above: *Choose a collar and fit it carefully if you want your cat to carry identification or a "key" to the catflap.*

An unneutered female can become pregnant even while she is still a kitten, at around six months old, so it is wise to start planning to have your kitten neutered at or around four to six months old.

Male animals wander great distances, establishing territory and looking for females. During these patrols they are likely to fight with other males, which puts them at risk of injury, and of picking up a number of infectious diseases that can be fatal. They are also likely to spray and mark more indoors, and are not great pet material. Most people who want pet cats should also neuter their male animals at four to six months old.

behavior problems

One of the aims of this book is to try to explain the fundamental nature of the cat, its natural behaviors and motivations, and to try to understand why it behaves as it does. We can watch and enjoy our cats while they are indoors with us in pet mode and while they are outdoors in wild mode. However, it is when some of these natural behaviors start to occur in the wrong place—for example, soiling indoors or scratching the furniture— that we must try to understand what has triggered this change in behavior, and how we can influence the environment and the cat to bring things back to normal.

One of the main reasons cats make such popular pets is that they carry out their toileting activities outside or confine them to a litter box within the house. Cats do not smell like their canine cousins—even when they are wet they do not smell musty and they seldom come in with muddy feet!

left: *If we can understand our cats' natural behavior we are more likely to solve their problems if they occur.*

right: *Problems can arise when cats do not get along and become aggressive with one another.*

Aside from leaving a few hairs on the furniture, pet cats do not usually sully the house, either with odors or damage. Thus when we start to notice the smell of cat urine in the house, or when the wallpaper or carpet is ruined by scratching, we can feel very let down by our cats. However, most owners realize that cats don't behave in this way to reap revenge or to annoy them—the motivation comes from something the cat perceives as a threat and it is reacting in the only way it knows. Feline reaction is, of course, very different from human reaction. However, we can understand that we too would react, albeit very differently, if we felt fearful or threatened.

Behavior problems are often described as normal behaviors occurring in the wrong place. They can be grouped into several different categories—indoor marking, which includes spraying and scratching; breakdowns in toileting behavior (urinating or defecating inside the house); aggression; nervousness; strange eating habits; and overgrooming. Each can have a different cause—some are problems from early kittenhood, while others are caused by changes to the cat's environment or management.

marking problems

Cats will mark indoors and outdoors but usually in different ways—indoors they rub scent on furniture and may

below: *A cat soiling indoors. Should your cat do this, check its physical health first, as this could be a sign that something is wrong.*

scratch carpets; however most of these marking behaviors leave no smell that is discernible to the human nose, and no visible marks, so we are quite happy to live with them. For the cat they provide security and familiarity, and a feeling of "home" or "den." Outdoors, cats will scratch, rub, and spray to mark the areas they frequent.

Spraying is not usually carried out indoors, so why do some cats, after years of "cleanliness," begin to behave indoors as they do outdoors? Spraying is performed standing up and results in a small volume of urine being squirted backward onto vertical surfaces (see page 34). When we smell urine in the house we need to try to differentiate between urination (usually done in a squatting position), and spraying, because the motivations are usually completely different.

Indoor spraying can be triggered by various things. If cats are entire (unneutered) sexual hormones can have a great influence on behavior—toms and queens in call or season spray indoors because their motivation to find mates is so strong. However, by neutering our pet cats we remove these overwhelming urges and they do not usually spray indoors (although they may still spray outdoors), so neutering is always a good first step if this has not been done.

Indoor spraying is usually a sign that the cat is feeling stressed or insecure, and is attempting to make itself feel more confident in its environment. While the inside of the house may previously have been regarded as safe and not requiring further definition, the cat now feels that it needs to be marked and reclaimed because of some threat—owners must try to ascertain what the threat might be. Common causes include: a new cat in the home;

neighboring cats coming into the house and perhaps marking in the house; fear of going outdoors because of aggressive cats; disruptions to the household, such as renovation or redecorating; new carpets or furniture; or even a new baby or person in the house. These disruptions can cause the cat to need something extra to make itself feel secure—the fact that we do not understand the messages it is trying to leave are as apparent to the cat as his behavior is to us! By getting upset we only make it feel more worried.

We need to "think cat," to try to improve the cat's security. How this can be done depends on the motivation for the behavior and thus finding the cause. However, even if this is not obvious there are still things that can be done.

threats from other cats

If you feel there is a threat to your cat from other cats outdoors, and they may even have been coming into the house, you can help your cat feel more confident by closing the catflap and letting it in and out yourself, or fitting a selective type that keeps other cats out. Chase other cats out of the yard and generally assist your cat when it is outside. When it feels that indoors is secure it will feel less need to mark it.

right: *There may be many hidden signals and stresses between cats of which we are unaware.*

new resident cat

While it may not be too difficult to prevent neighboring cats from coming into the house, the problem may also be caused by a new cat in the household. Perhaps the spraying cat does not get along with the new cat—this is the most likely cause—or it may be that the relationship of the resident cats (if there are several) has changed and a delicate truce has come to an end because of the additional cat.

redecorating and renovations

A cat is more likely to feel the need to mark if there are changes to its environment that it feels unable to cope with. This may be because it is a nervous feline that cannot deal with any small upsets within the house, or it may be because there are major disruptions going on. A cat kept entirely indoors may be very sensitive to changes in its indoor territory (such as smells brought in on feet) because it is not used to dealing with any type of threat.

When we redecorate our homes or replace the furniture, we inadvertently remove all the cat's scents, which it has placed to help it feel secure, and we replace them with strong-smelling

carpets, chairs, etc. New carpets, chairs, and paint smell strong even to the human nose, so they must be quite overwhelming to the scent-oriented cat. It may be worth keeping the cat out of the new room for a little while, if possible, until the new smells are not quite so strong and have mingled with the home's familiar smells.

above: *A male ginger-and-white alleycat showing prominent facial disc.*

below: *Some nervous cats hide on top of or under furniture and seldom venture outside.*

cleaning up

Part of the intricate process of passing on messages using scents is that, as they degrade, the cat is attracted back to them to re-mark. So, if we want to stop marking behavior, we need to remove not only the external cause but also the motivation to re-mark the area as the scent disappears.

This can be done by washing the area and then scrubbing with disinfectant. Leave until dry, or dry with a hairdryer, and try to keep the cat away from the area until it is dry. Obviously keeping the cat away for a couple of days will help let the smell dissipate and help break the habit. Leaving food at the site (for example, dry food stuck into an old margarine tub) may help prevent the cat from using that spot again, but if you have not removed the threat and thus the motivation to spray, the cat may simply do it somewhere else. If it has merely become a habit and you have managed to remove the threat, you stand a good chance of solving the problem.

avoid punishment

Never punish the cat—this will make it feel even more insecure. You must be seen as security for your cat, not an additional threat.

improving security

Cats rub their faces and bodies around their home to give it a "feeling of home" for them. We are beginning to understand these marking behaviors a little better than we used to—in fact there is a product now available from veterinarians that is based on the facial pheromones cats produce and aims to reduce spraying by making the cat feel secure. You can also help the cat

yourself by taking a cotton cloth and rubbing it gently around the cat's face then onto furniture and walls in the room where the cat is kept most frequently, and where it is spraying— this makes the cat feel less insecure and less likely to need to spray. You may need to restrict your cat's access within the house and concentrate on making it feel secure in one or two rooms.

By trying to ascertain what is upsetting the cat and combining all of these methods to improve its feeling of safety and security you may be able to solve the spraying problem.

above: You may want to prevent your cat from walking on kitchen surfaces and stovetops, for reaons of hygiene and for the safety of your pet.

scratching indoors

Scratching has different functions, the most obvious of which is keeping the claws sharp for hunting. However, this behavior cannot be solely for claw sharpening because the cat does not strop its back claws, yet they remain almost as sharp as the front ones.

below: Hunting—whether it is a mouse or a ball of string, is a cat's basic drive.

left: Cats have lots of energy and curiosity. They need an outlet for their natural behavior.

left: *Provide a scratch post for your cat so that it can sharpen its claws indoors.*

right: *Play is all part of practice for hunting. Indoor cats can become frustrated if they cannot fulfill these needs.*

of paper all over the floor. It may have an additional benefit in that owners suddenly start to take notice and give the cat attention, albeit angry attention. Some cats scratch more in the presence of other cats, suggesting that the display may also have an element of threat or at least "showing off."

When cats feel vulnerable they will utilize their ability to produce scents to "furnish" the room with their own choice of smell in an effort to make themselves feel more secure. While they may not resort to spraying in the house, they may use the scents produced by scratching to do this.

what else can you do?

First of all realize that the cat is not doing this out of spite or to cause destruction on purpose. Part of the art of remedying the situation is trying to decide why the cat is scratching.

The other purpose is to leave a physical and scent mark for the cat and for other cats. Secretions of a watery sweat from between the cat's pads leave a scent message on top of the physical marks.

Scratching is usually carried out outdoors, and there are several reasons why cats scratch inside our homes as well as outdoors. Indoor cats with no access to the outside still need to exercise the scratching behavior as part of their natural instinct. If you do not provide a scratch post (and maybe even if you do) they may choose an item of furniture or the carpeted stairs.

In addition to scent marking, another reason may be boredom or curiosity—some wallpapers are especially tempting because they are padded or raised, and once tampered with will permit an exciting game of paper removal, and a bonus game of chasing the little pieces

below: *Flight is the cat's natural reaction to threat. The nervous cat will spend a lot of time running from perceived danger.*

including string/sisal, bark, and carpet-covered. Cats like to scratch certain textures. For this reason there may be a slight danger in providing a scratch post covered in carpet—if the cat decides that this is the texture it enjoys, it may use the carpet around the rest of the house as well (just as putting newspaper in the litter box could endanger all newspapers left on the floor).

When you first get the post place it in front of the area that the cat is currently using and gently wipe the cat's paws down the post to leave some scent and show the cat what to do. Cover the other areas the cat uses (you can get guards for stairs), or use foil to protect them so you can divert its attention to the post.

If the cat has been scratching off the wallpaper you need to try to give it another outlet for its energies and curiosity. If you are redecorating, bear in mind that cats seem to like paper with raised textures—perhaps it would be better to use a flat paper or to paint the area. Don't encourage the cat by giving it attention when it is scratching.

Is it simply that you need to provide an outlet for claw sharpening in the form of a scratch post? Choose a post that allows the cat to stretch up and scratch as it usually does outside—there are many types available,

right: *If your cat starts to mark indoors, try to establish what might be upsetting it.*

messing in the house

Occasionally, cats have an "accident" and urinate or defecate inside our homes. For the meticulous cat that ordinarily uses the yard or outdoors this is very unusual and may just be a one-time problem—perhaps it was frightened, sick, or got shut in and couldn't use its usual site. For others it can be a sign that its usual toileting behavior has somehow broken down and for some reason it is using the indoors as a latrine.

One of the first things to do is to check that the behavior is not caused by a medical problem. Cystitis or some type of urinary tract disease or blockage may cause the cat to strain to

left: *In the wild the cat has to be self-sufficient by about five months old, so its energies will be directed toward learning to hunt.*

pass urine, or to feel the need to go little and often—the irritation caused by the problem making it go where it is, rather than getting to the litter box or outdoors. A stomach upset causing diarrhea can have a similar effect, although this is usually more noticeable, of course. Watch your cat and check where it is urinating—if it is squatting regularly and depositing small volumes of urine that are blood-tinged, have it checked by your vet. It may well have an infection or cystitis.

If you have deduced that there is no medical reason for the behavior, you need to try to find out what has motivated it. Don't punish the cat—this will only make it more fearful and likely to continue the behavior in secret.

avoiding going out

There can be several reasons why cats may not want to go outside to urinate

or defecate. An older cat may not want to venture out in bad weather, or it may be having problems with a stiff or frozen catflap. There may be something frightening outside that the cat does not want to encounter—perhaps another cat, a neighborhood dog, or a busy road. Remember that cats dig holes, squat over them, and then cover up—they can feel very vulnerable during this behavior sequence.

You can check out the catflap or provide a litter box for bad weather days if you have an old or weather-shy cat. If you think that the problem is caused by other cats frightening your cat outdoors or coming into the house, try to make your cat feel more secure by shutting the catflap and letting it in and out yourself to help it to feel protected. Changing to a selective catflap so that intruders can't come in may also help.

above: *Nervousness may be the result of a lack of early socialization or a trauma while a kitten.*

litter box problems

If you have a cat that has until now used a litter box but has suddenly started to go elsewhere in the house (usually somewhere hidden such as behind the couch or under a table), there may be an obvious reason. The cat may not like the litter to become too soiled, and you need to clean it out more regularly. Provide a covered litter box for extra security—even an inverted cardboard box with a hole cut in it may suffice initially. Clean out the litter box regularly so that it does not get too dirty. If you have several cats provide one litter box for two, or even one for each.

left: *Once trained to use a litter box as a kitten, your cat should not soil elsewhere indoors. Lapses in toilet training can usually be attributed to disturbances in the home or a new type of litter.*

The cat may refuse to use the litter box because you have changed the type of litter you buy—if so you may want to try some different types of litter to coax the cat back into using it. Usually the finer-grained and more sand-like the litter, the more the cat will want to use it. Never put food near the litter box—cats like their toilet and eating areas well away from each other.

Occasionally a cat decides not to use a box because it has had a bad experience—sometimes owners "catch" the cat on the box to give it pills or treatment and unknowingly create a bad association with using the box. Perhaps a new or existing pet or child has upset the cat and it feels insecure using the box—repositioning the tray and controlling the problem-causer may help.

place the tissue in the litter box so that the cat learns to make the associations you want it to. The cat may get the idea within a few days, or it may take a couple of weeks. When you think the cat has gotten the idea, let it out into the rest of the house gradually, one room at a time, where you can still oversee it and prevent accidents from happening.

marking behavior

Occasionally cats urinate or defecate as a marking behavior in the same way that they spray. This often occurs when owners go on vacation and leave the cats at home to be fed by a neighbor or catsitter. The cats decide to urinate on the bed—the place that smells most

strongly of their owners. This is probably because the cat's routine has been upset and an unfamiliar person has taken over the role of their owner (cats are often said to have a kitten/mother relationship with people so you could say that "Mom" has gone away). They urinate in a place where they can associate the smell with that of their owners. The best way to cure this is to keep the bedroom door shut.

Marking with feces, or "middening," is done by many mammals. Some cats will use the ploy outdoors, leaving feces uncovered on lawns or even up on walls where it can really be noticed; others do it indoors. The problem can be treated in the same way as other marking behaviors, such as spraying.

back to basics

If the various suggestions above do not work, it is worth considering confining the cat to a kittening crate or pen with its bed and a litter box. Sometimes there seems to be a breakdown in the learning process and it is worth taking cats back to basics—the way their mother taught them—and let them relearn to associate the litter with toileting.

Even when cats are only a few weeks old they are taught not to soil on their bed (by a couple of weeks old they move away from the nest to deposit waste). In a pen there is little option so they have to use the litter. You should try to bond the cat back to using the litter as a latrine. Let the cat out when you can oversee it and put it back in the box if you see it heading for a soiling point or behaving as if it is looking for someplace to urinate or defecate. If an accident does happen, clean up and

right: *Most cats don't like to have their stomach tickled and will bite or scratch in return.*

taking care of your
cat's health

above: *Bilateral third eyelid protrusion may be seen with a number of specific diseases.*

The basis of a happy relationship between cat and owner is reinforced by taking responsibility for its health. Ensuring their requirements for food and shelter and freeing them from infection and disease, further cements the bond between you.

left: *A plasticized wire cage is ideal for transporting cats to the veterinarian.*

choosing a veterinarian

Unless transportation is a problem, most people have a choice of veterinary clinics to attend within a reasonable distance of where they live. It is sensible to choose a clinic carefully—you will need to take your cat for annual examinations and/or vaccinations, as well as for any illnesses, and it is important that you develop a trusting relationship with your veterinarian.

Many factors will determine which veterinary clinic you decide to attend. Perhaps most important is word of mouth and recommendation from a friend or colleague you trust.

You can contact local clinics and find out about their costs for various routine procedures (for example, vaccination and neutering), but these costs are likely to vary widely. To some extent, costs of procedures at different clinics reflect the varying level of equipment available. Although most (but not all) clinics possess an X-ray machine, some also have ultrasound, endoscopes, blood pressure monitoring, or other more specialized equipment.

In addition to equipment, some clinics are staffed with veterinarians with specialist qualifications—for example in internal medicine, dermatology (skin diseases), ophthalmology (eye diseases), or orthopedics. Most veterinary clinics will be happy to tell you what kind of equipment they have, and what, if any, specialists work there. Some clinics also schedule open houses where you can look around and meet the veterinarians.

You may also want to see if there is a feline-only clinic in the vicinity. With the ever-increasing popularity of cats as domestic pets, there are an increasing number of feline veterinary clinics being established, and the American Board of Veterinary Practitioners offers vets a specialist qualification in feline practice.

transporting your cat

Taking your cat to the vet can be a traumatic experience, both for the cat and for you. It is always safest to transport your cat in some form of secure basket or carrier. Many different varieties of carriers are available, but one of the best and most practical is the white wire basket. These baskets have a hinged lid, making it easy to put the cat in and get it out again, they are rigid and secure, and they allow the cat to see out clearly.

If you have traveled by car and have

left: *If you are unsure of your cat's ailment, or what remedy the vet prescribes, then ask him/her a question. He or she will be happy to allay your fears.*

above: *The health of your new kitten is in danger from a variety of diseases and infections. A primary vaccination at nine weeks is vital to ward off this danger.*

a very nervous or easily frightened cat, it may be best to leave the cat in the car (in the basket) until the vet is ready to see you. Some cats will get very apprehensive if they have to sit in a waiting room with noisy dogs, or even with other cats.

pet insurance

It is possible to take out insurance against the cost of investigation and treatment of illness or injury for your cat. Many insurance companies offer this service, which involves paying an annual or monthly fee to obtain the coverage. This type of insurance is becoming increasingly popular, due to the potentially high costs of veterinary treatment, and your veterinarian can provide advice on suitable companies and policies.

second opinions and referrals

While many cats maintain good health throughout their lives, some inevitably develop significant diseases. Sometimes these diseases can be very complex and, if difficult to diagnose and/or treat, as in human medicine, your veterinarian may recommend referral to a specialist or a university clinic. Referral to a specialist or another veterinarian for a second opinion is always possible and can be at the owner's request, as well as at the suggestion of the veterinarian.

above: *A lot of veterinary clinics actually allow their customers to view their premises during open house, making owners more at ease when leaving their pet.*

right: *If you are still concerned about your cat's ailment after visiting a vet, never be afraid to ask for a second opinion, or to visit a feline specialist.*

when to go to the vet
signs of ill health

As with humans, cats can develop a wide variety of different illnesses. However, the signs of disease may vary from very subtle to very dramatic.

nonspecific signs of illness
Your cat may simply seem out of sorts—quiet, inactive, and appearing depressed or irritable. Vague, nonspecific symptoms such as these may be transient and resolve themselves without any veterinary attention, but if they persist for more than a few days, it is important to have your cat checked by a vet. Although the signs may be vague, they can sometimes indicate a serious underlying disease that requires investigation and treatment.

Similarly, if your cat loses its appetite and stops eating, this should not be allowed to continue very long before veterinary treatment is sought. In general, if your cat goes without food for more than three days, even if he or she appears quite bright, veterinary attention is needed since serious adverse effects can occur from lack of food intake.

Either a noticeable gain or, more commonly, a loss in weight can indicate a serious underlying disease and is a reason to take your cat to the vet. It was once thought that protrusion of the nictitating membrane (third eyelid, or *hoares*) was a nonspecific sign of illness and/or weight loss in cats. In fact, it is now recognized that a number of specific

left: *An unwell tabby male cat lying hunched. Spotting early signs of ill health through abnormal behavior can prevent a disease or infection worsening.*

above: *Plastic carriers and covered litter boxes are better for transporting your cat, since they are easily cleaned and disinfected once used.*

diseases can cause this so, again, if your cat's third eyelids remain protruding over the eyes for more than a few days, this should be checked by a vet.

specific signs of disease

With many diseases, specific clinical symptoms may develop that make you aware that there is something wrong, and these may make the nature of the illness obvious. Diseases associated with the respiratory tract, for example, may result in sneezing, coughing, wheezing, or difficulty breathing. Gastrointestinal disease may cause constipation, diarrhea, and/or vomiting. Kidney disease may result in an increased thirst, and bladder inflammation (cystitis) may cause an increased frequency of urination, and straining to pass urine. All these are relatively common clinical signs of illness in cats.

It may sometimes be difficult to decide whether veterinary attention is necessary, or if the signs relate to a minor ailment that may resolve itself. For example, one of the common causes of diarrhea is dietary indiscretion—eating spoiled food. In such cases, the diarrhea usually settles down within a few days without the need for any special treatment. In general, if the cat remains bright and appears well in other respects, it is usually safe to wait two or three days before seeking veterinary attention.

There are some exceptions to this rule, though. Some symptoms can indicate a serious underlying problem that requires urgent veterinary treatment. For example, a cat that is vomiting persistently and is unable to

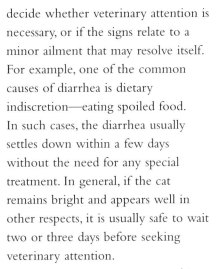

above: *Siamese cat with protruding membranes. Always have your vet examine any physical injuries or infections to the eyes.*

keep down any food or fluids, a cat that develops heavy or labored breathing, and a cat that is straining to pass urine without producing anything are all examples. If you ever have any doubt about the necessity for veterinary attention, the safest option is to speak to the vet on the telephone—he or she will be able to advise you appropriately.

It is very important not to be tempted to give your cat any human medicines. Although it may seem appropriate sometimes (for example, giving painkillers if the cat appears lame), cats are unusually sensitive to a variety of different drugs, and can suffer severe and even fatal toxic reactions. Only administer medicines that have been prescribed by your veterinarian.

left: *Elderly cats naturally need more attention to prevent illness. Regular check-ups with the veterinarian are required to maintain good health.*

preventive **health** care

Preventive health care is about trying to prevent your cat from becoming ill, or seriously ill, and it takes many forms. The most important aspects of preventive health care are routine vaccinations against common infectious diseases, regular worming, preventive flea treatments, annual veterinary examinations, and neutering your cat.

worming

Tapeworms and roundworms are two of the most common intestinal parasites of cats. Tapeworms are long, flat worms composed of many individual segments, whereas roundworms are much shorter and have rounded bodies.

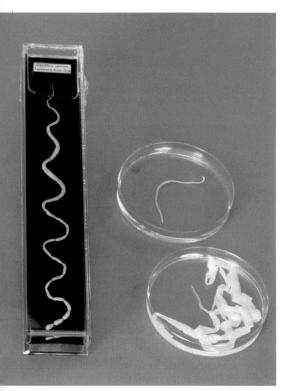

Roundworms produce microscopic eggs that are shed in the feces, whereas tapeworms release visible segments (containing eggs) in the feces that sometimes look like grains of rice. They can occasionally be seen on the hair around the anus of the cat.

Roundworms (most commonly *Toxocara cati* and *Toxascaris leonina*) are very common, particularly in young cats and kittens. Eggs passed in the feces can be ingested (eaten) by another cat, leading to transmission of infection. In addition, the eggs may be eaten by another animal (the "intermediate host") such as a mouse, and a cat can also be infected by preying on (eating) the infected intermediate host.

Toxocara cati infection can also be passed on to kittens through the milk of the queen (mother), explaining in part why infection is so common in kittens. Roundworm infections are extremely common, and it is best to assume that *all* kittens will be infected.

Many different tapeworms can infect cats, but the two most common are *Dipylidium caninum* and *Taenia taeniaformis*. Flea larvae eat the eggs of *Dipylidium* (shed in the feces of an infected cat), then other cats become infected with this tapeworm by ingesting (eating) an infected flea

left: *Intestinal worms*—Dipylidium caninum *(left), a roundworm (top right), and a* Taenia *tapeworm (bottom right).*

during grooming. As flea infections are so common, this tapeworm is also common and it should be assumed that any cat with fleas will also have *Dipylidium* infection.

In contrast, rodents (rats and mice) eat the eggs of *Taenia taeniaformis* so other cats become infected during hunting by eating an infected rodent. Infection with this worm is less common, but should be expected in any cat that actively hunts.

Hookworm may also be found in cats although in some regions they tend to be much more common than in others. Hookworm infection occurs through ingestion of their eggs. They cause disease by attaching themselves to the intestinal wall and ingesting blood, resulting in signs such as anemia and weight loss. Infection is more common in adult cats.

Regular worming of cats is important, both to eliminate the worms for the cat's health, but also because there is a very small risk that some of these worms (e.g., *Toxocara cati* and *Dipylidium caninum*) can infect humans—although this only occurs extremely rarely. Kittens require regular worming for roundworms from around four to five weeks of age until they are four to six months old. Following this, cats should generally be wormed every three to twelve months, using a preparation active against roundworms, tapeworms, and hookworms. Many different

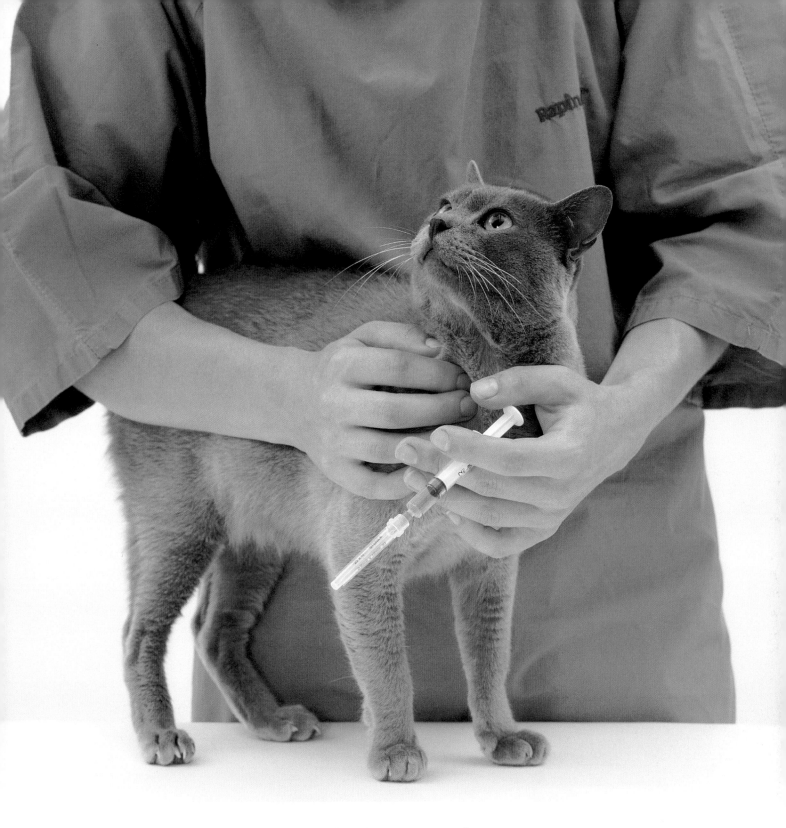

preparations are available for this, but it is best to seek advice from your veterinarian, as he or she will have access to safer and more effective wormers than are available in stores.

vaccination

Regular vaccination is a very important part of preventive health care for cats. A number of different vaccines are available, but the most important of these are rabies, panleukopenia, and the cat "flu viruses" (feline calicivirus—

FCV, and feline herpes virus—FHV). These diseases are discussed in more detail later (see section "Infectious Diseases"). In some countries, vaccination against rabies is a legal requirement.

All cats should also be vaccinated against panleukopenia, since this is a widespread virus and causes an often-fatal gastroenteritis. Vaccination against FCV and FHV should also be routine for all cats, since these flu viruses are so common, and again the disease can

above: *A blue Burmese cat about to be given booster vaccination. Note needle covered for safety until ready for use by the vet.*

be very severe. The frequency with which vaccines are administered depends on a number of factors, but cats are generally vaccinated every one to three years.

Other cat vaccines are available in many countries (e.g., for the virus that causes feline infectious peritonitis, and for feline leukemia virus). However, since these viruses are not so widespread in the cat population, and since not all cats are necessarily at risk of developing these infections, your veterinarian will be able to advise you whether such vaccines are necessary for your cat.

As in humans, a mild reaction (being not up to par for a couple of days) is quite common after vaccinations, but if your cat develops any reaction you are concerned about, contact your veterinarian immediately.

heartworm

Infection with heartworm (*Dirofilaria immitis*) is seen in cats in many parts of the world. Infection in cats is less common than in dogs as cats are naturally more resistant to it. Transmission of heartworm is through mosquito bites. Heartworm infection

can cause heart, lung, and brain disease. In areas where heartworm infection is relatively common, cats can be given medication to prevent infection.

neutering

Unless a cat is going to be used for breeding, it is usually safest to have it neutered at a young age. This has several advantages: it avoids any unwanted pregnancies, it helps to prevent unsociable behavioral characteristics from developing (particularly in male cats), and it averts the development of medical problems associated with the reproductive tract.

Cats can be neutered at virtually any age, but it is most commonly done when they are kittens at around four to six months of age, ideally before they reach sexual maturity. The operation is simple in both the male and the female, but requires a general anesthetic and therefore a short stay at the veterinary clinic.

fleas

Fleas are a ubiquitous problem throughout the world, but are particularly prevalent in warm, humid climates. Even in temperate climates, the use of heating furnaces in homes provides a warm environment ideal for the flea to breed.

Adult fleas (which are wingless insects) spend part of the time on the animal (dog or cat), where they bite and suck blood, and part of the time in the environment (e.g., the house and yard). Cat fleas can also bite humans, but although their bite may be irritating, these fleas cannot live on humans. The adults will shed eggs in the environment, which hatch into larvae and initially feed on organic debris, then pupate before becoming adults.

It is almost impossible to prevent cats

left: *Cats can be neutered at any age, though it is best to have it done before they reach sexual maturity.*

right: *Spraying a cat with a non-aerosol flea spray. A cat that is excessively licking its coat may have fleas or ticks.*

inset: *Fleas and "flea dirt" collected from a cat.*

from becoming infected with fleas, but although some cats develop severe skin irritation in response to the flea bite, others can have large numbers of fleas without showing any obvious signs. Careful inspection of the skin, or grooming using a flea comb, may be necessary to detect flea infection, but often the most noticeable sign of fleas is the presence of "flea dirt" in the cat's coat or bedding. This flea dirt looks like small black or brown granules, and is actually the digested blood that the fleas have passed.

In recent years, a number of safe and highly effective flea treatments have been developed that can control flea infections. Again, it is best to seek advice from your veterinarian as he or she has access to the safer and more effective products available, and can advise you on what is most appropriate for your circumstances. In general, treatment involves using a preparation to kill fleas that are on the cat (commonly this is administered as a liquid, dropped onto the skin), and also a preparation to kill fleas in the environment (house), which is commonly in the form of a spray.

annual examinations

Regardless of whether your cat has vaccinations every year, or less frequently than this, it is a good idea to have an annual examination with your veterinarian. This provides an opportunity to discuss any problems you have with your cat, and also allows the vet to give the cat a thorough clinical examination, thereby potentially detecting problems at an early stage, and allowing effective treatment before they become too severe.

practical **help** with your **cat**

giving pills

Many forms of medication for cats need to be given in pill form. Unfortunately, giving pills to cats often proves quite a challenge. For all but the most experienced pill-giver, this should be regarded as a two-person job. Having your cat adequately restrained by a helper will make the process much easier, and it enables you to concentrate on getting the pill in the right place, without having to worry about the claws.

The helper should try to concentrate on keeping the cat's body and legs still by gentle but firm restraint. Although you certainly won't want to cause any discomfort to your cat, it is equally important that the restraint be firm

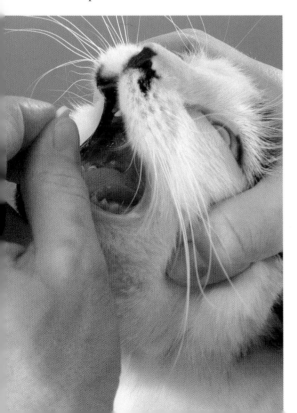

left: *Giving a tablet. The head is held firmly with one hand while the mouth is opened with the other, then the tablet is dropped at the back of the tongue.*

right: *Administration of ear drops. The base of the ear should be massaged afterward to work the solution well in.*

enough to prevent the cat from wriggling too much. With firm restraint, most cats submit to the inevitable.

While the body and legs are being restrained by a helper, you can then hold the head firmly in one hand, using the fingers of the other hand to open the mouth. The pill can be dropped at the back of the tongue, using a small utensil such as a pencil to push the pill to the back of the mouth, if necessary. It is important to try to get the pill as far back in the mouth as possible (right at the back of the tongue). From here, the pill can only be swallowed, and you are not left with the frustration of your cat turning around and spitting the pill out after several minutes of hard work.

Some people find "pill-giver" gadgets (available from pet stores or veterinary clinics) helpful to get the pill to the back of the mouth. Other tricks to get the cat to swallow the pill include shutting the mouth, holding the head up, and stroking the throat gently, and trickling a little water into the mouth using a spoon or syringe immediately after dropping the pill on the tongue.

Don't despair if you find giving the pills difficult at first—everyone does. With practice, though, it can be done quite easily and, if you are having difficulties, your veterinarian will be able to help show you how best to do it.

giving eye and ear drops

Eye and ear infections often have to be treated by administration of drops or ointment. As with giving pills, it is important to use gentle but firm restraint to avoid injury to your cat or the people holding the cat. Again, it is extremely useful to have two people,

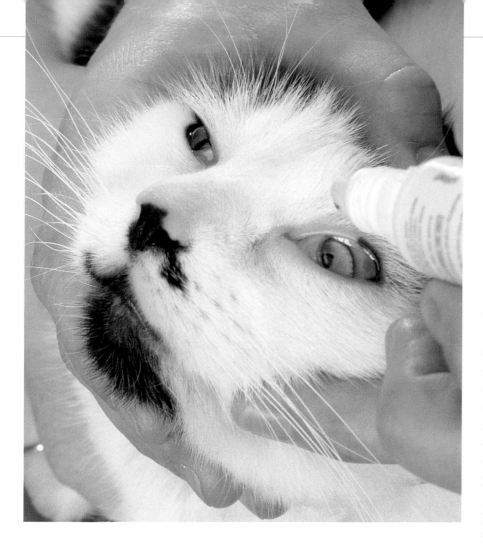

one to restrain the body and legs, the other to administer the eye or ear medication.

For eye drops, the head must be held firmly, tilted upward, and then, from just a short distance, the liquid can be dropped directly onto the surface of the eye. Inevitably your cat will blink, and it may shake its head. Some of the eye drops will run off the eye onto the surrounding fur, but this is normal.

Eye ointment can be a little more difficult to administer. While restraining the head, the eye has to be held open and the ointment squeezed onto the surface of the eye or onto the inside of the lower eyelid. You will need to follow carefully your veterinarian's instructions as to the quantity of drops/ointment to be applied, and the frequency of administration.

Giving ear drops involves holding the head and ear firmly with one hand, and putting the drops into the opening of the ear canal. Before letting go of the head, it is useful to massage the area below the opening of the ear to work

the ear drops all the way down the ear canal, which is shaped like a sock.

clipping nails

Most cats keep their claws well-sharpened, and regular nail clipping may be done to remove the sharp tips and thereby reduce the damage done to furnishings (or people). Occasionally,

some cats fail to keep their claws sharp, and they may grow excessively long, also necessitating regular clipping.

Although your vet will be happy to do this job for you, it is something that can be done easily at home, providing you have a good pair of sharp clippers (available from your vet or from pet stores). Having a second person to restrain the cat will again help, and the ends of the nails can be carefully clipped one by one. The tips of the nails contain no nerves or blood vessels, and therefore this is not in any way uncomfortable for your cat. However, there is a central part of the nail (the quick) that does have both blood vessels and nerves, and it is important not to cut the nails too far back so that this area is exposed. Fortunately, in cats this is usually easy to see, and therefore easy to avoid when cutting the nails.

below: *The clear, sharp point of the cat's claw can be clipped without any risk of injury or pain.*

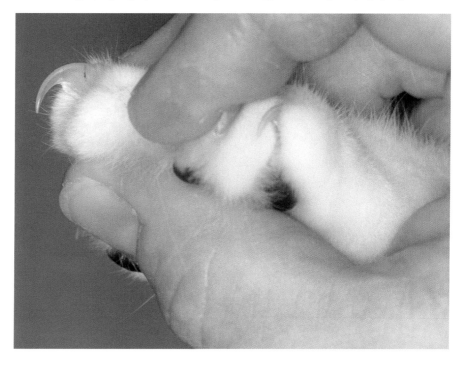

accidents and emergencies

burns

Fortunately, burns are uncommon in cats. They may be caused by spillage of hot material (for example, boiling water, oil, or fat), contact with caustic chemicals, or electrical contact. Depending on the severity, there will be variable damage to the skin, which may result in complications, such as fluid loss and secondary infection.

The initial treatment of burns is aimed at keeping the skin cool and moist by the application of cold water or ice. Veterinary attention is important to assess the degree of damage to the skin, and thus the most appropriate treatment. Before reaching the vet, it is helpful to keep a cloth soaked in cold water over the burned area of skin. Severe burns require intensive care, and can be fatal.

road traffic accidents

Road traffic accidents are one of the most common causes of injury to cats, and are an inevitable consequence of giving cats the freedom to wander outside. If you know your cat has been involved in a road traffic accident, even if he or she is showing no overt signs of injury, it is still important to get the cat checked by a vet as soon as possible. There can sometimes be severe internal injuries that would otherwise go undetected until dramatic and perhaps fatal signs develop.

In other cases an overt injury is present that requires obvious treatment.

There is a common misconception that it is better not to move a cat after a road accident, and that the vet should be called out. However, since there is no such thing as a paramedic service for cats, it is best to carefully put the cat in a car and transport it to the veterinary clinic. The vet will diagnose the extent of the injuries and provide appropriate treatment at the clinic.

Two conditions requiring immediate treatment before transporting the cat to a clinic are severe bleeding and breathing difficulty. If there is heavy bleeding from a wound, the flow of blood should be stopped immediately by applying a tight bandage to the wound (see also "cuts and wounds" below).

With breathing difficulty, it is vital to ensure that there is no obstruction to the flow of air in the mouth or nose. If there is obstruction to airflow due to accumulation of fluid or blood, this should be carefully wiped away to try to relieve the problem. Almost all other accident injuries will require treatment and attention from your veterinarian.

drowning

Although most cats don't enjoy water, drowning is uncommon since, if necessary, most cats can swim quite well. If a cat has almost drowned, urgent veterinary attention is clearly required. However, as an immediate measure, it can be helpful to hold the cat upside down (suspended by its back legs) and gently swing the cat from side to side. This will help to drain any water from the lungs and may help to stimulate the breathing.

heatstroke

Heatstroke can occur when cats are confined in hot spaces (typically in a closed car on a hot, sunny day). The signs of heatstroke include panting, distress, vomiting, collapse, and unconsciousness. Cats with heatstroke have a high body temperature and treatment involves reducing this temperature and combating the shock (circulatory collapse) that can occur.

Treatment for shock usually involves administering intravenous fluids, but you can help to reduce the body temperature immediately by soaking the cat in cold water, and transporting it to the vet wrapped in towels also soaked in cold water.

cuts and wounds

Due to their inquisitive nature, cats will often come home with cuts or lacerations. Commonly these are caused by contact with objects such as broken glass, aluminum cans, and barbed wire. Treatment for these cuts depends on their severity, how recent the wound is, and how much tissue damage there is. Fresh, clean wounds

right: *Panting and breathing difficulties can indicate severe respiratory problems in cats, and should not be ignored—see your vet immediately.*

can often be sutured by your veterinarian, allowing rapid healing. Other wounds have to be left open to heal, or bandaged. Antibiotics are often necessary to prevent infection, or to treat established secondary infection.

If a cut or wound is bleeding heavily, it is important to stop the bleeding before you take your cat to the vet. Applying pressure to the wound with a finger for a few minutes can stop small amounts of bleeding.

With heavier bleeding, it may be necessary to place a pad over the wound (gauze or cotton wool) and tie a bandage tightly around the wound to apply constant pressure.

If wounds are contaminated with dirt, wash this out carefully with plenty of clean water, if your cat will allow you, and try to prevent the from cat licking the wound, since this will cause further damage. When cleaning a cut or wound, don't be tempted to use a disinfectant

solution, because this often causes further damage to the delicate tissues.

bites

Cats carry a number of nasty bacteria in their mouths. Whenever a cat bites, the penetrating wound from the teeth result in bacteria being deposited under the skin of the animal (or human) receiving the bite. Bite wounds should therefore be carefully cleaned with clean water or salt water

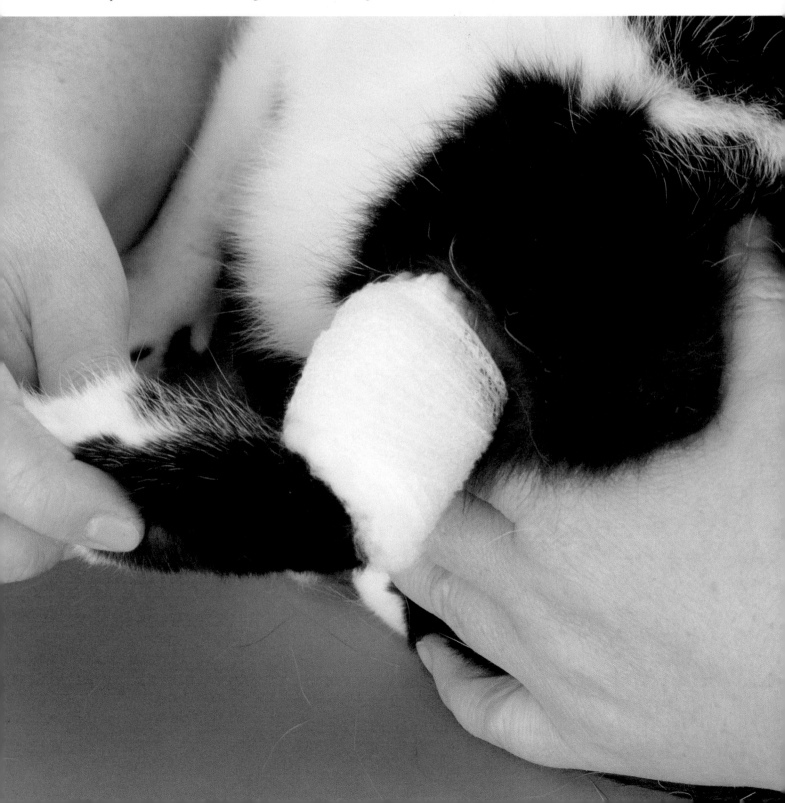

(approximately a teaspoon of salt to a pint of water). This will sting and could cause an aggressive response. The wound needs to be inspected carefully for several days. If it is very tender or begins to swell noticeably, this usually indicates that infection has occurred and that veterinary treatment is required.

below: *A bandage wrapped firmly around a wound is useful to stop any bleeding.*

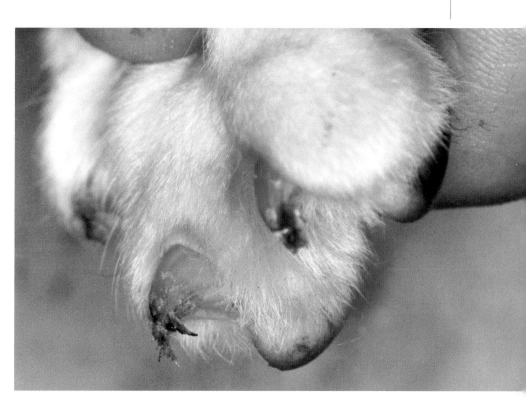

poisoning

Cats metabolize drugs and chemicals differently from many other animals, and this makes them highly susceptible to poisoning. Chemicals that would not cause problems in humans or other animals can be toxic to cats, and although poisoning is uncommon (because cats are very fastidious about what they eat), it may occur by accidental exposure or incorrect administration of medications.

It is of great importance that you never give cats any medication other than that specifically prescribed by your veterinarian, or sold specifically for use with cats. If you are ever in doubt, always contact your veterinarian first for advice.

Never be tempted to give your cat products designed for use in humans or other animals, as this can cause serious problems. For example, cats are extremely sensitive to many analgesic drugs, and even a small dose can be fatal. It is also very important not to overdose cats with medications, so, for example, when treating with a flea product, don't be tempted to give more than the recommended dose. The additional medication may not increase

above: *Frayed claws are a common sign that a cat has been in a road traffic accident.*

the effectiveness of a product, and may cause toxic side effects.

Cats are also susceptible to poisoning with a number of disinfectants (most notably the phenolics). In general, hypochlorite (bleach) disinfectants are among the safest and most reliable for use around cats, although again, care needs to be exercised to avoid direct contact with the product, which can be irritating.

Cats are sensitive to the toxic effects of many organic compounds, and if your cat has petroleum tar products spilled on its coat, it is important to remove them quickly. Cooking or vegetable oil can be used to soften the product if necessary, before thorough washing with a mild detergent and plenty of water.

If you know your cat has swallowed some pills that could be toxic, it may be possible to induce vomiting to try to prevent absorption of the product. Giving a small quantity of hydrogen peroxide or very salty water is often effective in inducing vomiting prior to seeking veterinary attention.

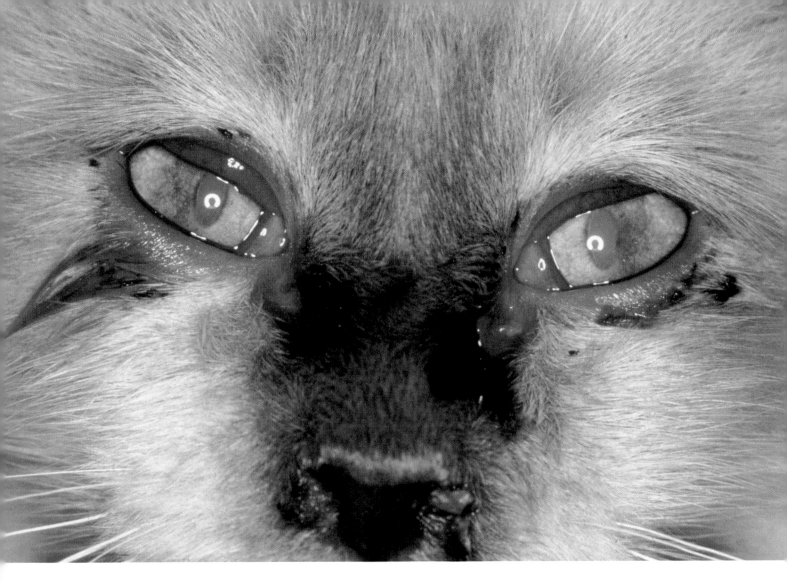

infectious diseases

upper respiratory tract infections (cat flu)

Cat flu is a common disease in cats of all ages and can be particularly severe in very young and old cats. The vast majority of cases are caused by infection with feline herpes virus (FHV), feline rhinotracheitis virus, and/or feline calicivirus (FCV).

Affected cats develop symptoms similar to heavy colds and flu in people. There is often eye discharge (due to conjunctivitis) and sneezing with sometimes heavy nasal discharge. Mouth ulcers can develop, and the discomfort and inability to smell may cause cats to stop eating. Affected cats are often dull and depressed, with a raised temperature. Without treatment symptoms usually abate in two to three weeks but some cats are left with chronic nasal discharge or eye disease. Deaths following respiratory virus infections are rare, but can occur, particularly in untreated cats and kittens.

Specific antiviral treatments are not generally available for cat flu. Prompt veterinary treatment is very important to combat secondary bacterial infection (which is a major cause of worsening clinical symptoms) and to stimulate eating and drinking. Your cat can be encouraged to eat and drink by using strong-smelling foods, such as fish in oil, and warming the food gently to body temperature. The eyes and nose can be gently bathed with warm water to remove secretions. Severely affected cats may need intravenous fluids and more intensive supportive treatment in a veterinary clinic.

above: *Severe nasal and ocular discharges are typical signs of cat flu.*

Vaccines are available to protect against cat flu and their routine use is recommended due to the ubiquitous nature of these viruses. However, although vaccination helps to prevent severe symptoms from developing, it does not necessarily prevent cats from becoming infected, and they may still develop mild disease. The viruses responsible for cat flu are susceptible to most disinfectants, and only survive a few days in the environment.

feline leukemia virus (FeLV)

FeLV is one of the most severe viral infections of cats, and is a common cause of illness and death. Typically,

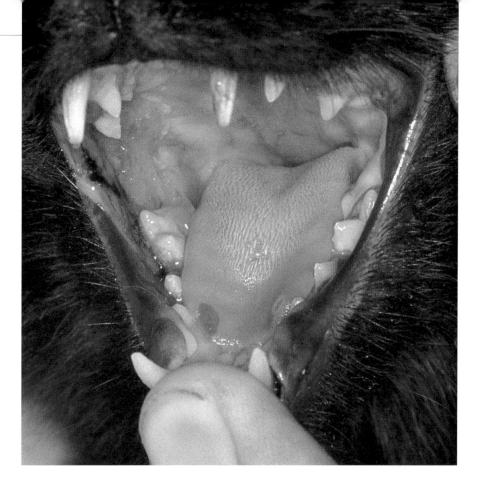

around 1 to 2 percent of the cat population is persistently infected with this virus, but infection is more common in colonies of cats, where as many as 30 percent of the cats may be infected with the virus.

As its name implies, FeLV is able to cause neoplasia (cancer) of the white blood cells (leukemia), but in addition, the virus also causes the development of solid tumors (lymphomas) at various sites in the body.

Although the development of these tumors is common in infected cats, other diseases may also develop. In many infected cats, there is a profound suppression of the immune

system, leading to increased susceptibility to a wide range of secondary infections that would not normally cause a problem. These cats develop a variety of clinical symptoms and may have a progressive deterioration in their condition over time.

A severe and fatal anemia is another common sign of FeLV infection, and occasionally the disease may cause

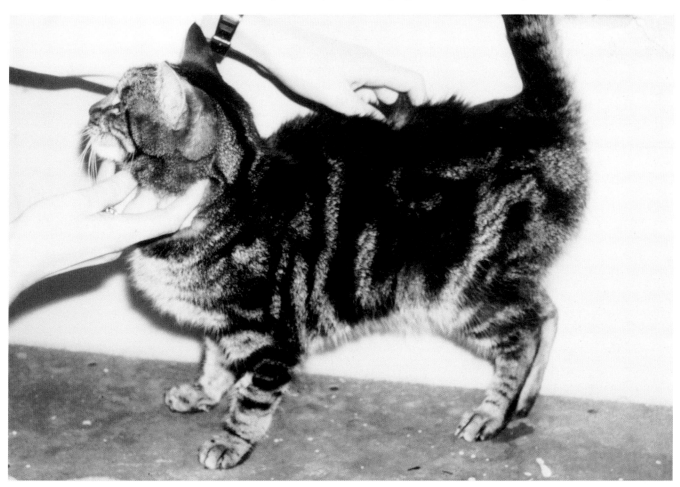

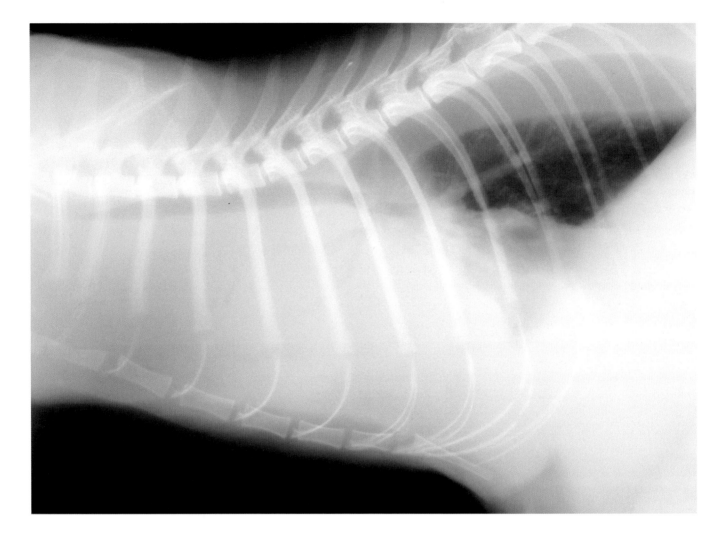

abortion, severe enteritis (resulting in diarrhea), neurological (nervous) problems, and ocular (eye) disease. FeLV is thus a significant disease of cats, and around 80–90 percent of infected cats die within three to four years of the diagnosis being made.

The virus cannot survive longer than a few hours outside the cat, so infection is transmitted via direct contact between cats. An infected cat sheds large quantities of the virus in saliva, but the virus is not highly contagious so it generally takes prolonged close contact between cats, involving mutual grooming and sharing of food bowls, to allow transmission of the virus.

Not all cats exposed to FeLV develop persistent infections (and thus develop FeLV-related diseases). Many cats mount an immune response to the virus that successfully eliminates it from the body. However, these cats

sometimes experience a transient infection with the virus, and there may be a period of several weeks or months during which the virus remains dormant in the body (latent infections) while the immune response is eliminating it completely. Only cats that are persistently infected with the virus are at a high risk of developing FeLV-related disease.

Diagnosis of FeLV infection is relatively easy, and can be done through a blood test performed by your veterinarian. Unfortunately, there is no specific treatment for FeLV infection. Nevertheless, although most infected cats eventually die of FeLV-associated disease, many respond to symptomatic and supportive treatment from your veterinarian, at least for a period of time.

Vaccines are now available to help protect cats against FeLV infection, and their use is highly recommended in any

cat that goes outside and therefore has contact with other potentially infected cats. The vaccines are not 100 percent reliable, however, and it is important not to deliberately expose a vaccinated cat to FeLV, for example by allowing it to mix with or housing it with a known infected cat.

feline infectious anemia (FIA)

FIA is an uncommon disease caused by an organism called *Haemobartonella felis* that attaches itself to the cat's red blood cells. Infection may lead to damage to the red blood cells, leading to their destruction. This can result in anemia, with typical signs of weakness, collapse, pale tongue, poor appetite, and, in severe cases, difficulty in breathing.

Diagnosis of FIA has been difficult and dependent on identifying the organism microscopically using special stains. However, new tests are being developed that may make diagnosis much more reliable. If infection is identified, cats can be treated with antibiotics to control the infection (although response to treatment is variable). Other drugs may be useful to prevent destruction of the red blood cells, and in severe cases, your veterinarian would be able to give a blood transfusion.

feline infectious peritonitis (FIP)

Feline infectious peritonitis (FIP) is an uncommon disease of cats caused by infection with a virus. FIP is a fatal disease, and is more common where large groups of cats are kept together. There are many different strains of the virus, which differ in their ability to cause disease. Most cats are probably infected by direct contact with other cats, since the virus does not survive long in the environment. Most individual cats exposed to feline viruses will not develop disease (the strain of virus will not cause FIP, and/or the cat will eliminate the virus by development of a good immune response). However, those that do develop disease almost invariably die.

The first signs of illness with FIP may be very vague—depression, poor appetite, and raised temperature. Within a few days or weeks, other signs usually develop, including accumulation of fluid in the abdomen or chest, leading to a swollen abdomen, or difficulty breathing, and/or inflammation at various sites including the eyes or the brain. When disease develops, rapid deterioration is common.

FIP is very difficult to diagnose as there is no reliable blood test. The current blood tests available show whether a cat has been exposed to a virus, but the vast majority of cats exposed to these viruses do not develop FIP. Therefore, a positive test does not mean that the cat has FIP. Currently the only way to confirm a diagnosis is by microscopic examination of affected tissue by a pathologist at a laboratory.

FIP cannot be treated effectively after it has developed, but a preventive vaccine is now available in many countries. However, as with FeLV, the vaccine does not give complete protection against disease, and its use is often only recommended in high-risk situations.

below: *A very pale color to the gums and membranes in the mouth may indicate anemia.*

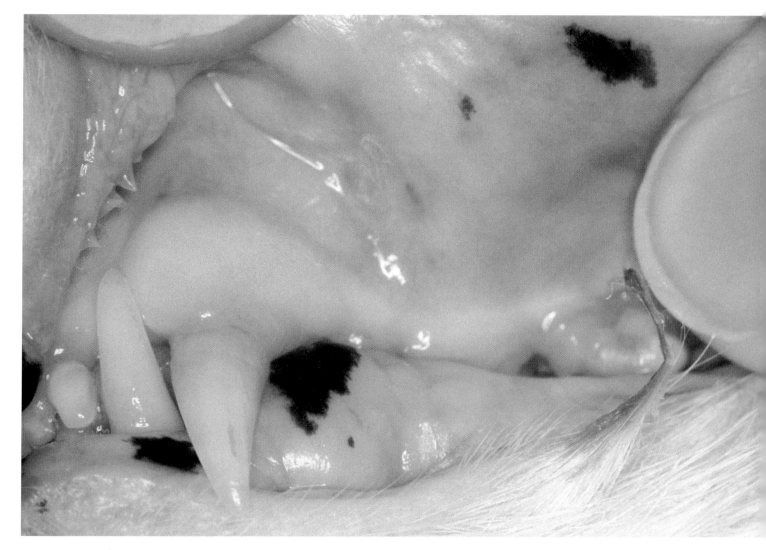

125

Unvaccinated cats are highly susceptible to infection with this virus, which commonly causes a fatal disease. The virus targets rapidly dividing cells, typically those lining the intestine and also the bone marrow. It can cause very severe enteritis that may manifest as acute vomiting, or vomiting with diarrhea (often with blood in the diarrhea), or even sudden death. Affected

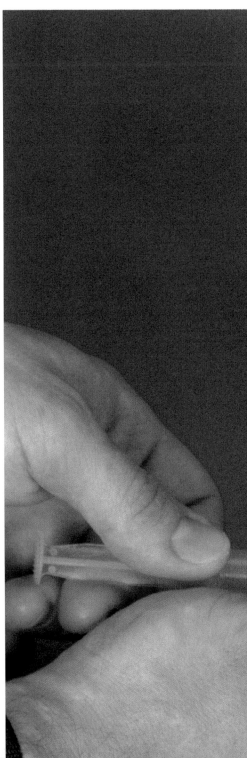

feline immunodeficiency virus (FIV)

FIV is the feline equivalent of HIV. The viruses are from the same family and cause progressive disease through impairment of the immune system. Although they are very similar viruses, there is no risk of FIV being transmitted to humans.

FIV is another virus that is very fragile and cannot survive in the environment. Like FeLV, the virus is present in the saliva of infected cats, but it generally requires direct injection of the virus through biting for a cat to become infected. Infection is therefore much more common in free-roaming, aggressive male cats. Normal social interactions such as mutual grooming have a very low risk of transmitting FIV.

Once a cat is infected with this virus, it is probably impossible to get rid of the infection. However, not all cats necessarily develop disease.

In those that do, FIV usually causes a progressive, debilitating disease with a variety of different clinical symptoms, including inflammation of the gums and mouth, weight loss, poor appetite, fever, swollen lymph glands, vomiting, and diarrhea.

Diagnosis of FIV is usually achieved through a simple blood test, although sometimes additional testing is required because the blood test is not totally reliable. Although no vaccine is available for FIV, clinical signs may improve with supportive and symptomatic treatment (including antibiotics for secondary infections) from your veterinarian, and some cats may respond to human anti-HIV drugs such as AZT.

feline panleukopenia

Feline panleukopenia is caused by infection with feline parvovirus. This is a highly resistant virus that is widespread in the environment.

cats may die despite aggressive veterinary treatment including intravenous fluids and antibiotics. In addition to the enteritis, infected cats often develop a severe depletion of their white blood cells (due to the virus replicating in the bone marrow) that effectively suppresses their immune systems and makes them vulnerable to secondary infections. In young kittens, the virus can also attack the nervous system.

No specific antiviral agents are available to treat infections, but fortunately vaccination against this infection is highly successful and strongly recommended for all cats.

rabies

Rabies is caused by a virus, and is widespread throughout the world. It is of major importance because the virus can be transmitted to humans. The virus is usually maintained in populations of wild animals (foxes, skunks, and raccoons), where it can be transmitted to domestic animals mainly through bites. The virus spreads to the brain where it can cause distress, timidity, excitement, aggression, salivation, paralysis, and death. There is no treatment for rabies after symptoms occur, and death is inevitable. In areas where rabies is present, vaccination is recommended, and in many places compulsory. The available vaccines are highly effective.

below: *A blood sample may be needed from your cat to investigate and diagnose the underlying disease.*

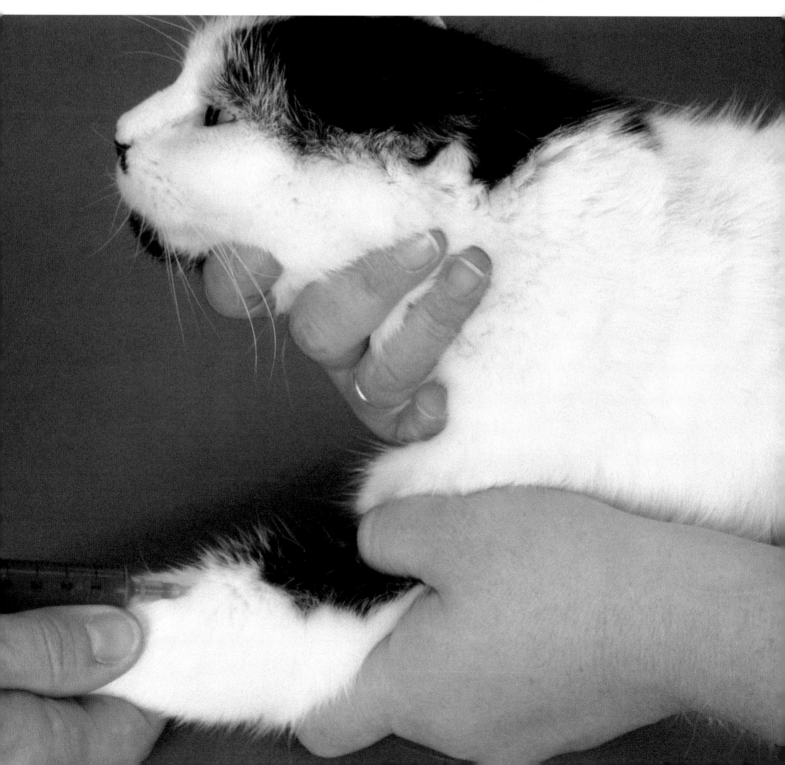

common **problems**

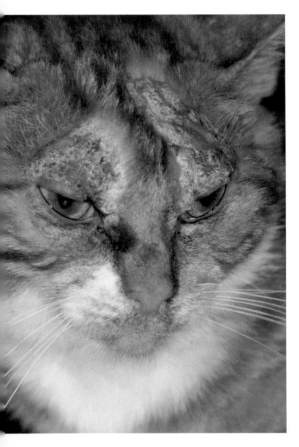

vomiting and diarrhea

Diseases of the stomach and intestinal tract may cause vomiting and/or diarrhea. Sometimes these symptoms occur with diseases of other body systems. Cats vomit quite readily, and occasional vomiting in an otherwise healthy cat may not be abnormal. It is also normal for cats to periodically vomit hair balls, which are accumulations of hair swallowed during grooming.

Many cases of vomiting and diarrhea resolve themselves. Commonly your cat may have eaten some spoiled meat or other material that has caused irritation to the stomach and intestine, and within two or three days the symptoms will stop. However, if the vomiting or diarrhea is more persistent or very severe (frequent vomiting or passage of diarrhea can readily cause dehydration), veterinary attention is needed. Persistent symptoms that are accompanied by any weight loss also need to be investigated.

Observations that help to indicate whether the vomiting or diarrhea is serious include: the timing of symptoms (for example, whether vomiting occurs every time the cat eats); if the cat shows other signs of illness (for example, depression, lethargy, or generalized pain); if the cat stops eating; if there has been any weight loss; and if there is any blood in the vomit or diarrhea.

Symptomatic treatment is usually tried for mild cases of vomiting and diarrhea. This usually involves withholding food for 24 hours then providing a simple diet (such as boiled fish or chicken) for a few days in small quantities. Water should be freely available to avoid dehydration. Your veterinarian may also prescribe drugs to help stop the vomiting or diarrhea. If the signs are severe, or a serious underlying problem is suspected, other investigations may be needed. Hospitalization may be required to give intravenous fluids. Further investigations that are recommended vary depending on what the veterinarian suspects as the underlying cause. Typically this may include blood tests (checking for viral diseases, and kidney and liver problems), X rays, endoscopy (examination of the stomach and intestine through a flexible viewing tube, passed through the mouth under a general anesthetic), and possibly exploratory surgery.

constipation

Constipation is an accumulation of feces that results in difficult bowel movements. There may be reduced frequency or absence of defecation, and your cat may strain to pass feces without being able to, or small amounts of very hard, dry feces may be produced.

Constipation may be caused by many factors, and in most cases simple treatment (altering the diet, administering enemas, and providing medication to help passage of the feces) resolves the problem. Some conditions predispose cats to recurrent episodes of constipation, for example hair balls in longhaired cats, strictures (narrowing) of the large intestine, and pelvic injuries (for example, after a road traffic accident), which can result in nerve damage or narrowing of the pelvis.

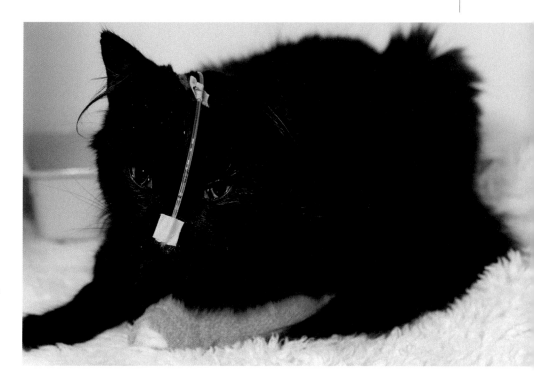

Occasionally, older cats also develop a condition called "megacolon" where the muscle layers of the large intestine lose their ability to contract normally, thus making passage of feces difficult. Diagnosis of these more complicated causes of constipation may require X rays and other investigations. Treatment is also more difficult, and some cats have to be on persistent medication to control the constipation, or may even need surgery.

Never be tempted to use any human preparations to treat a constipated cat—some of these are dangerous for cats. Only use products recommended or prescribed by your veterinarian.

dental disease

Dental disease is one of the most common conditions seen in cats. The most frequent problems seen are due to periodontal disease (inflammation around the tooth root) and gingivitis (inflammation of the gums). Cats do not develop true dental cavities as humans do, but they can get painful erosions of the teeth, known as "neck lesions."

Common signs of dental disease are a loss of appetite, evidence of pain or

below: *X ray of a cat with heart disease, showing a very enlarged heart. This mainly affects the older cat.*

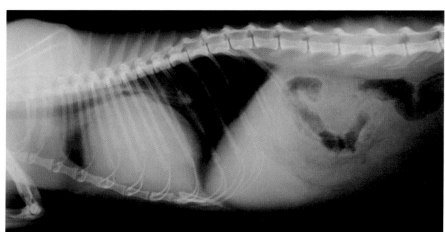

discomfort when trying to eat, excessive dribbling (sometimes with blood), and an unpleasant odor to the breath. Accumulation of bacterial plaque on the tooth surface, which leads to development of tartar (calculus) on the tooth, is a common cause of dental disease in cats, as in humans. Tartar is brown in color, and usually first seen at the edge of the gum. In severe cases, it covers the entire tooth surface. The accumulation of tartar ultimately leads to infection around the tooth and the typical signs of dental disease. As with humans, some cats seem more predisposed to developing dental disease than others.

A regular veterinary examination (every 6 to 12 months) is strongly recommended to detect dental disease at an early stage. Early detection with appropriate treatment may lead to full recovery, whereas, if the condition progresses too far, some teeth will have to be removed. Treatment of gingivitis and periodontal disease generally involves cleaning and polishing the teeth under a general anesthetic. Antibiotic therapy may also be required where there is significant infection.

Some cats develop severe gingivitis with no or minimal signs of accompanying dental disease. The inflamed areas may extend beyond the gums to other areas of the mouth, but the exact cause of this disease is not yet fully understood. Some cases may be an exaggerated inflammatory response to dental tartar. This condition is often very difficult to control and may require repeated or constant treatment.

Keeping the mouth and teeth clean is the main method of preventing dental disease. Regular inclusion in the diet of foods that encourage chewing (for example, tough pieces of meat) help to keep teeth clean by the mechanical action of scraping plaque and tartar from the teeth. Regular

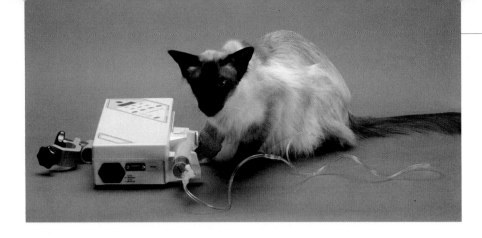

above: *Intravenous fluids may be needed if a cat gets dehydrated.*

brushing of the teeth is probably the single most effective way to keep the teeth clean, and a number of toothpastes and brushes designed for use with cats are available from your veterinarian or pet store. With gentleness, patience, and perseverance it is possible to regularly clean some cats' teeth in this way, but not all cats tolerate it.

heart disease

In dogs, the most common form of heart disease involves the valves between the four chambers of the heart. If these become diseased they can become "leaky," and ultimately result in heart failure. Cats also get heart disease, but this usually involves disease of the heart muscle itself rather than the valves, a condition known as cardiomyopathy.

In the early stages of heart disease, many cats show no signs of illness at all. They may adapt to reduced heart function by modifying their behavior (that is, less activity), but the changes may not be at all obvious. An early indicator of underlying heart disease may be abnormal heart sounds or an abnormal heart rhythm detected by your veterinarian during routine clinical examination.

Most cats with heart disease ultimately develop heart failure that may cause breathlessness or difficulty breathing, and profound lethargy. There may also be an accumulation of fluid in the chest or, less commonly, the abdomen. Another complication

that develops in some cases is thromboembolic disease. In these cases, blood clots form spontaneously in the heart, and may be washed out in the bloodstream and block the blood supply to areas of the body. Most commonly this involves the blood supply to the back legs, resulting in the sudden onset of severe pain and paralysis of the hind limbs.

The diagnosis of heart disease by your vet involves tests such as X rays, ultrasound, and electrocardiogram (ECG). Blood tests may also be needed to rule out certain underlying causes of the heart condition. Many cats with heart disease respond very well to treatment, particularly if the disease is detected before overt heart failure has developed. However, if thromboembolic disease develops, this is usually a very bad sign and many cats do not recover from it.

chronic nasal discharge and sneezing

Chronic upper respiratory tract (URT) disease is a relatively common problem in cats. The most common cause is chronic postviral rhinitis (nasal inflammation). In this condition,

previous viral infection (cat flu—see page 120) results in permanent damage to the delicate lining of the nose, but the persistent signs of sneezing and nasal discharge are due to secondary bacterial infection of the damaged nasal passages. Other potential causes of persistent sneezing and discharge include fungal infections, inflammatory polyps, and tumors.

With typical cat flu it is important that cats receive proper treatment to try to avoid the long-term problems that can occur with severe nasal damage. Where signs of persistent (that is, several weeks' duration) sneezing and discharge are present, your veterinarian will probably need to do some investigations to rule out other possible causes of the discharge (he may try X rays, examination of the nose under anesthetic, or culture swabs from the nose). Sometimes, collection of biopsies may be necessary to confirm a diagnosis.

If chronic, postviral rhinitis is diagnosed, long-term treatment is often necessary. However, because of the initial viral damage to the nose, while signs can usually be controlled with treatment, recurrent infections are likely to require further treatment in the future. Treatment usually consists of antibiotic courses, possibly combined with drugs to help clear the mucus

below: *Gingivitis (inflammation of the gums) is a common problem in cats.*

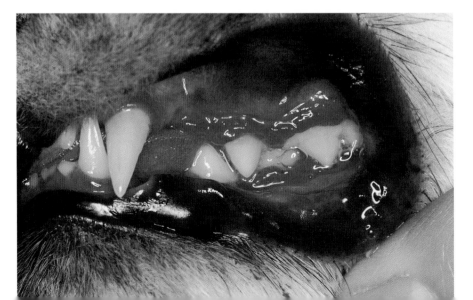

from the nose. Steam inhalation can be very useful—for example, keeping the cat in a hot, steamy bathroom while you take a bath or shower may help to relieve some of the congestion.

coughing in cats
Coughing usually results from inflammation or irritation of the airways in the lungs. Coughing can occur for a variety of reasons, including the presence of foreign material in the airway (for example, pieces of inhaled grass), or irritation from inhaled liquids or gases. Infections such as cat flu or pneumonia may also cause coughing, but one of the most common causes of persistent coughing in cats is chronic bronchitis. In this condition, there is inflammation of the small air passages, but usually a specific cause of the inflammation is not found.

It is normal for all cats to cough occasionally and, if the cough is nonproductive and the cat is otherwise well, this is unlikely to require treatment. However, if the cough persists for more than a few days, is severe, or if the cat appears unwell, veterinary attention should be sought. X rays are often useful in determining the cause of the cough. If chronic bronchitis is present, it may be very difficult to cure, but the coughing can usually be controlled with appropriate treatment.

conjunctivitis
Conjunctivitis is inflammation of the delicate membrane that surrounds the eye, forming a seal with the inner surface of the eyelid. The third eyelid is also covered by conjunctiva. With conjunctivitis, this membrane becomes reddened and sometimes swollen. There is usually a discharge from the affected eye(s). Conjunctivitis can affect one or both eyes.

Conjunctivitis can be caused by trauma from cat fights, foreign bodies such as grass seeds, exposure to irritant chemicals, and a variety of infections

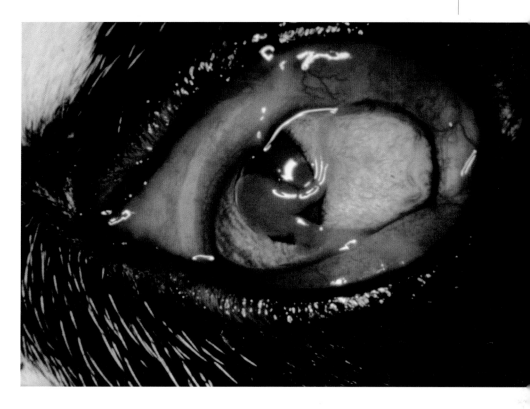

above: *Severe conjunctivitis with inflammation and ocular discharge.*

(mainly viruses and bacteria). Most cases of conjunctivitis clear rapidly with appropriate treatment from your vet (for example with anti-inflammatory and/or antibiotic eye drops). Some cases of conjunctivitis are more persistent, particularly with some of the infectious agents, and your vet may need to take eye swabs to determine the cause of the inflammation and select the most appropriate treatment.

In some longhaired cats, a clear eye discharge may be a normal feature. Due to their flattened faces, these cats can have poor tear drainage from the eyes, leading to an overflow of tears and eye discharge.

kidney disease
The main function of the kidneys is to remove waste products from the bloodstream and excrete them from the body in urine. Unfortunately, cats are particularly prone to developing disease of the kidneys, especially in old age, that results in chronic renal (kidney) failure.

Early signs of disease can be very nonspecific, including weight loss, loss of appetite, and poor coat quality. As the disease progresses, other signs

may develop, including an increase in thirst and the volume of urine produced, intermittent vomiting and diarrhea, generalized weakness, and oral ulcers. Kidney failure can be confirmed as the cause of these symptoms by your vet through analysis of blood and urine samples.

Unfortunately, once renal failure has developed, it is an incurable condition, and often results in a cat needing to be euthanized. However, with appropriate supportive treatment, many cats live for prolonged periods of time with this disease and maintain a good quality of life.

Treatment options for chronic renal failure are dependent, in part, on what complicating factors have developed. An altered diet (to reduce protein and phosphorus concentrations) is usually beneficial—commercial diets are available for this, or your vet can advise you on how to prepare such foods at home. It is important to encourage your cat to drink plenty of fluids, and for this it is better to feed wet (canned)

left: *Hair loss in a cat due to flea infestation. By using a non-aerosol spray one can quickly remedy this problem.*

foods rather than dry foods. If your cat prefers dry food, try soaking the kibble in water first. Your vet may prescribe other medications to overcome problems such as hypertension (high blood pressure), vomiting, weight loss, and poor appetite.

skin disease

Most skin disease in cats manifests itself as areas of hair loss and/or areas of inflammation of the skin. Sometimes skin nodules or lumps may also develop.

Fleas are by far the most common cause of skin disease in cats. The cat flea (*Ctenocephalides felis*) is also present on dogs, and it is virtually impossible to prevent cats from becoming infected, particularly if they go outside. You will not always be able to see obvious evidence of fleas because many cats groom themselves so well that presence of the fleas can be difficult to detect. Some cats become allergic to flea bites, and in these individuals just one or two flea bites can trigger intense irritation and inflammatory response in the skin.

Cats can also develop a number of other skin conditions, including mites, lice, and fungal infections (particularly ringworm); some cats develop hair loss through excessive grooming that may be due to a behavioral problem.

If you know your cat has fleas, your vet can advise you on the most appropriate way to control the problem. Most other skin conditions are relatively easy to diagnose and treat, although your vet may need to take samples of hair and scale, or even a skin biopsy, in order to be sure of the underlying problem.

cystitis

Cystitis is an inflammation in the bladder. It causes an increased frequency of urination, straining to urinate (sometimes with obvious discomfort), and sometimes blood in the urine. A common cause of this in

zoonoses

Zoonotic diseases are those transmissible from animals to man. Although such diseases are rare, you need to take precautions and be aware that there can be problems. Misinformation is often spread through ignorance or fear.

cat bites

Cats carry a wide range of bacteria in their mouths, and a cat bite commonly results in deposition of bacteria deep beneath the surface of the skin. These bacteria may then proliferate and cause a painful swelling or even an abscess. *Pasterurella multocida* is the bacteria most commonly involved, although there are many others that can cause problems. Bite wounds from cats should always be carefully washed, and if the bite wound is deep it is

always sensible to seek medical attention, since a course of antibiotics may be required. Medical advice should also be sought if any swelling, pain, or obvious infection occurs.

fleas

Fleas are extremely common on cats. Common cat fleas cannot survive on human blood, but they can bite humans and cause skin irritation. A variety of effective products are available for controlling fleas, and your veterinarian can advise you on the best products to use.

ringworm

Ringworm (dermatophytosis) is one of the most common zoonotic diseases derived from cats. Ringworm is a fungal infection of the skin, and the most common cause in cats is an

organism called *Microsporum canis*. In cats, ringworm usually causes small areas of hair loss, often with some scaling or crusting of the skin. However, the appearance of ringworm can be extremely variable. In humans, too, ringworm can cause patches of hair loss, but infection is more common on the arms, body, or legs, where circular patches of reddened skin are a common sign. A diagnosis of ringworm can be made by culture of the organism in the laboratory. If your cat is infected with ringworm, it can be successfully treated, but it is important to try to avoid excessive close contact with the cat and, ideally, to wear gloves when handling the cat, until the problem has resolved.

It is important to not let children have direct contact with ringworm-infected cats. Ringworm in humans can also be treated successfully with a variety of drugs but medical attention is necessary if you suspect this problem. Ringworm spores are shed into the

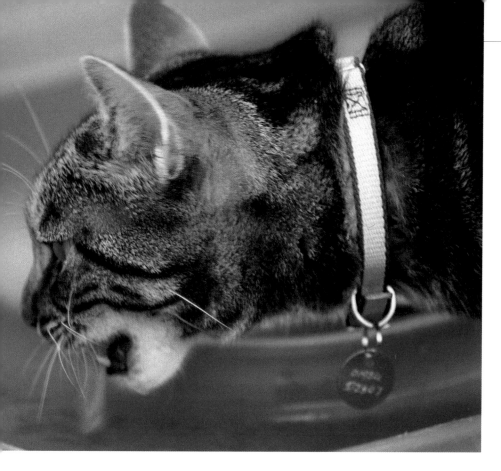

possible causes (through analysis of urine samples and bladder X rays). Where a specific cause is identified, appropriate treatment can be given, and a number of drugs are also available to treat the common sterile cystitis in cats. Many cases of sterile cystitis resolve in three to five days without any treatment, but if the symptoms recur frequently it is obviously sensible to have your cat checked out by your vet.

Also, if your cat is unable to pass *any* urine, despite repeated attempts, urgent veterinary attention should be sought, since this could indicate a complete blockage to the flow of urine. This is more common in male cats, and is a potentially life-threatening condition.

humans and dogs is a bacterial infection in the bladder. However, in cats this is an uncommon cause, and many cats have a form of sterile cystitis. Your vet will want to rule out infections and bladder stones as

environment from infected cats and are quite resistant. Thorough cleaning throughout the house, including regular vacuum cleaning and disinfecting where possible, is therefore recommended.

toxoplasmosis

Toxoplasmosis is a parasite that infects cats and many other mammals, including humans. It is primarily a concern for pregnant women since, if infection occurs during pregnancy, damage can occur to the developing fetus. Most human infections come from poor meat hygiene (handling uncooked meat or eating undercooked meat). However, for a short period after they are first infected with toxoplasma, cats may shed eggs (oocysts) in their feces, and this is another potential source of infection for humans. Because of this, it is recommended that litter boxes be emptied and disinfected on a daily basis (the eggs don't become infectious for humans until more than 24 hours

after they are shed in the feces), and that pregnant women not be involved in cleaning litter boxes.

intestinal worms

Very rarely, humans can become infected with a cat roundworm (*Toxocara cati*) or the tapeworm (*Dipylidium caninum*). These infections are very rare (canine roundworm infections are more common in people), but regular worming of cats for both roundworms and tapeworms is an important part of general health care.

campylobacter and salmonella

These are two intestinal bacteria that can cause severe gastrointestinal disturbances and can affect many animals, including humans. Infection in humans is usually through the food chain, and infection from cats is rare, although they can be a potential source. Routine hygienic precautions (for example, washing hands after handling a cat) should always be

followed, but particular care should be paid to handling cats with diarrhea. If the diarrhea is prolonged, severe, or contains blood, veterinary attention should always be sought to identify the underlying cause. If campylobacter or salmonella are identified, specific treatment and/or monitoring may be required.

cat scratch disease

Cat scratch disease (CSD) is a rare bacterial infection of humans characterized by swollen lymph nodes and sometimes other symptoms (for example, fatigue, muscle pain, sore throat) that can occur following contact with a cat in which biting or scratching has taken place. CSD is an uncommon disease and serious illness is very rare. The main organism responsible for this disease, *Bartonella henselae*, is quite common in cats, and transmission between cats probably occurs mainly through fleas.

extra care for the older cat

With improved nutrition and health care, more and more cats are living to greater ages. With advancing age, a number of changes occur in the body. Older cats tend to exercise less and have a lower metabolic rate, and because of this, unless their food intake lowers, they have a tendency to become obese. Conversely, dental disease is more common in older cats, and is a common reason for poor appetite in this age group, which may lead to weight loss.

Some of the common specific disorders seen in older cats are hyperthyroidism (a hormonal disorder), chronic renal (kidney) failure, dental disease, and neoplasia (cancer). Also, while younger animals usually have only one disorder at a time, older cats more commonly have a number of interacting disease processes. Old age itself is not a disease, but we need to pay particular attention to older cats, so that if they develop disease, we can recognize it and treat it early, and so uphold their quality of life for as long as possible.

It is important that elderly cats have easy access to a warm, draft-free bed, situated where the cat can sleep safely without fear of disturbance. It is advisable to feed older cats a highly

right: *Feeling for enlarged thyroid glands is a routine part of the examination a veterinarian will perform on an older cat.*

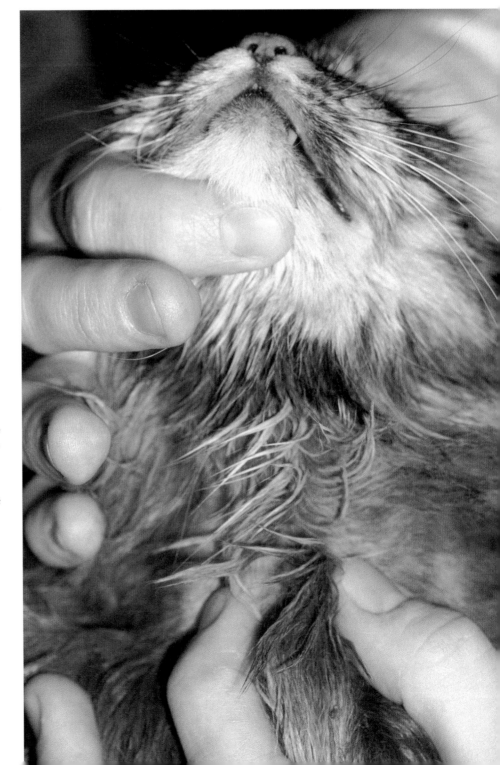

palatable, possibly reduced calorie diet, with a high water content. They should always have easy access to fresh drinking water. Easy access to an indoor litter box is advisable, to reduce the risk of "accidents" occurring.

It is important that elderly cats receive regular veterinary checks to detect any problems at an early stage, when treatment will be more successful. Annual examinations are recommended, and your veterinarian may recommend a series of blood tests at these times to help in the early detection of disease.

hyperthyroidism

Hyperthyroidism is the most common endocrine disease in cats. It is particularly common in cats more than eight to ten years of age, and commonly causes marked weight loss (although the appetite may be increased), abnormal thirst, and a poor coat. A benign enlargement of the thyroid gland resulting in excessive production of thyroid hormones causes the disease.

This disease is readily diagnosed by your vet, although a blood test needs to be performed to confirm the diagnosis. Treatment is usually very successful and very simple. It is possible to administer drugs to suppress the overactive thyroid gland and thus reverse the clinical signs. The disadvantage of this therapy is that the drugs have to be given daily or twice daily for the remainder of the cat's life to control the condition. Alternative treatments that overcome this disadvantage include surgical removal of the affected tissue under general anesthesia, and in some places facilities for a type of radiation therapy are available.

neoplasia

Tumors (neoplasia, or cancer) are quite common in cats, and although they can occur in cats of all ages, older cats are more prone to developing them.

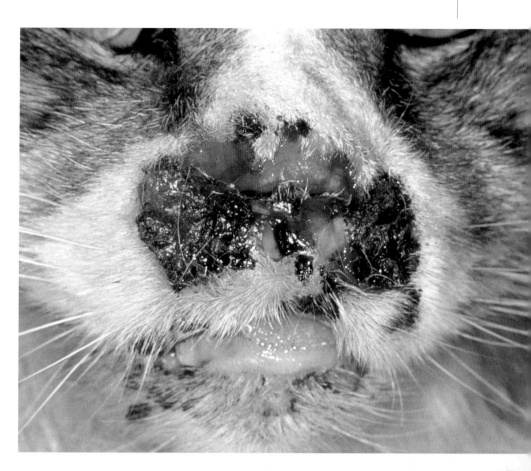

above: *Tumors, such as this skin tumor on the nose of a cat, are more common in old age.*

Unfortunately many tumors in cats are malignant, which can make treatment very difficult. Nevertheless, there have been many advances in the treatment of neoplasia in both humans and animals, and while there are some tumors that are still incurable, many may respond well to therapy.

Treatment options for tumors usually include surgical removal, the use of chemotherapy, or radiation therapy. The recommended form of treatment varies according to the type of tumor. Chemotherapy and radiation therapy can sound frightening, but lower doses of these agents are used in animals, compared to humans, to avoid the risks of severe side effects. This means that permanent remission of tumors is less common in animals, but nevertheless, treatment has the potential for inducing remission for many weeks, months, or years in some situations.

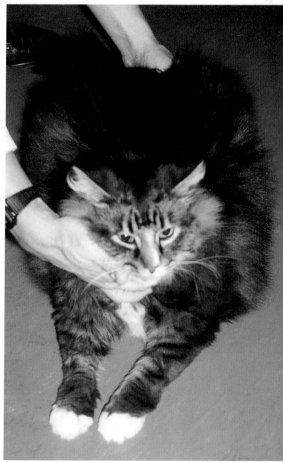

above: *Obesity can be a problem, particularly in older cats. Attention must be paid to diet and the ability to exercise as the cat gets older.*

saying goodbye

Regrettably, there are occasions when your vet may suggest that you should consider having your cat "put to sleep" or euthanized. This may occur if your cat has a terminal illness or is in chronic pain. Part of the privilege and responsibility of pet ownership is knowing and understanding when to put an end to unnecessary suffering. Inevitably, this decision is difficult, and the advice of your vet is frequently helpful in making this hard decision.

Although difficult, enabling your cat to die in peace, with dignity, and without further suffering, can be one of the kindest things that an owner can do for a suffering cat.

A cat can be "put to sleep" or euthanized by the vet, at home or at the veterinary clinic. Many vets will happily arrange an appointment at the clinic outside of normal consulting hours, so that the procedure can be performed quietly and privately.

The procedure itself is very simple, involving an injection of an overdose of anesthetic into a vein (usually a vein in the front leg). The cat loses consciousness within a few seconds, and this is rapidly followed by death. This is a controlled, quick, and painless way of performing euthanasia, and for most cats is completely stress-free.

left: *Grieving is natural after the death of your pet. Treasure your memories, and remember the good times.*

If you have a very nervous cat, your vet may recommend giving your pet a sedative to calm him or her down prior to euthanasia.

Whether an owner stays with the cat while euthanasia is performed, or leaves the cat with the vet, is entirely a choice for the owner, but one that is best made well in advance. If you choose to stay, try not to get too upset, as this may be communicated to the cat and cause distress.

After euthanasia has been performed, most vets are able to arrange cremation of the body, or alternatively, some owners prefer to take the body home for burial in their yard.

grieving for your cat

It is entirely natural to feel upset and emotional when your pet dies. Don't be afraid to show your feelings in front of the vet—he or she will understand. It also takes time to get over your loss. You may go through a mixture of emotions—sadness,

loneliness, and even anger. This is all quite normal and part of the process of coming to terms with your loss.

It is important not to feel guilty or blame yourself for your cat's death, and it often helps to talk to someone about your feelings. It is important to remember that the decision for euthanasia is usually reached only as a last resort, but inevitably as an act of kindness, to avoid suffering. Vets cannot always save a cat's life. Treasure your memories. Remember the good times and what you loved most about your cat.

Children may also have difficulty coming to terms with euthanasia. This may be a child's first experience with death, but it is important to be honest with them. Tell them the truth and encourage them to talk about their

right: Although it may be a difficult decision, ending your cat's suffering through euthanasia is sometimes the right option.

above: *Try not to feel guilty at the death of your pet. A vet cannot always save a cat's life, no matter how much it is loved by the family.*

feelings, and share your feelings with them. Talk openly about your cat, and try to concentrate on the good times. A new pet may help, but it is usually better not to get another cat too soon. You and your child will need time to get over the death of your old pet.

cat
breeds

above: The cream Tonkinese is one of the foreign shorthair breeds of cat — lively, playful, and good company.

This section lists all the major cat breeds and their various subsets, with some lesser known breeds on pages 178–181. The section concludes with useful information on showing (page 182) and breeding cats (page 186).

left: A litter of Ragoon kittens demonstrate how difficult it can be to breed a perfectly marked cat. Of three, only the one on the right conforms to the bi-color Ragoon standard, the others having too little white.

Abyssinian

The Abyssinian is one of the oldest distinct breeds—many of today's cats' pedigrees can be traced back for well over a century. Even in the nineteenth century, the origin of the breed was obscure; some maintained that it had been bred from imported cats, although from where was never quite clear; others said that it had been developed from domestic cat breeds.

Medium sized and of moderate type, neither cobby nor elongated, the Abyssinian is an elegant and muscular cat. With its moderate wedge head and large ears, which are often tufted, the Aby has a very distinctive look. The coat is short and close-lying and does not need much grooming, except when the cat is shedding.

One of the essential features of the breed is its ticked coat pattern, each hair having bands of light and dark color. The original color, known as usual or ruddy, has a deep rich orange undercoat with black ticking, giving a rich golden brown appearance, while the sorrel (formerly known as red) has a slightly lighter undercoat with cinnamon ticking for an overall look of burnished copper.

right: *This sorrel (red) Abyssinian shows the beautiful copper glow of its cinnamon ticking.*

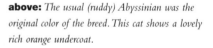

above: *The usual (ruddy) Abyssinian was the original color of the breed. This cat shows a lovely rich orange undercoat.*

Abyssinians are also bred in blue, chocolate, lilac, fawn, red, cream, and six tortie colors, plus silver versions of all of these, although not all of the colors are recognized in all countries. Although from the description and names such as "Aluminum" and "Silver Fancy" it is likely that silver Abyssinians were shown in the nineteenth century, they are still not universally recognized today.

The Aby is rather independent, can struggle if picked up or restrained when it does not wish to be, and is somewhat wary of strangers, although very friendly with familiar human companions. Although quite talkative, it is not noisy. Abyssinians are lively, energetic, and, given the opportunity, excellent hunters.

above: *The blue Abyssinian, a newer color, has a delicate oatmeal undercoat with blue ticking.*

American Curl

Originating from a strange curled-eared kitten found in California in 1981, the American Curl is now a recognized breed in the United States, although few are seen elsewhere.

A medium-sized cat, similar to a domestic long- or shorthair but less cobby and rounded than a pedigree British or American Shorthair, the Curl has one very distinctive feature: the tips of its ears curl backward. The degree of curl varies from a very slight tilt at the tip to a full 180-degree crescent, but should not curl around to touch the head.

American Curls are bred in both longhaired, with a semi-long, silky coat, and shorthaired varieties, and may be any color or pattern, since these are not important features of the breed. The longhaired Curl requires more frequent grooming than the shorthaired, but does not need the daily grooming of a Persian, since it lacks a thick undercoat.

A friendly and playful breed, the Curl is similar in temperament to a domestic cat and makes a good companion.

American Wirehair

Another breed of purely American origin, Wirehairs are descended from a cat found in New York in 1966. Since the unusual coat is caused by a recessive gene, American Wirehairs cannot be mated to other cats to get wirehaired kittens, so the breed is fairly uncommon and rarely seen outside the United States.

The American Wirehair is very similar to the American Shorthair in shape—a fairly cobby cat of medium size, with a rounded head and body. It is bred in all of the same colors and patterns as the American Shorthair, but is distinguished by its coat. Instead of smooth straight hair, the tip of each guard hair (the longer hairs in the coat) is bent, giving a rough, springy feel and a slightly untidy appearance.

The Wirehair requires little grooming and is a good companion, without displaying any extremes of temperament.

below: *An ordinary street cat? Close inspection of the coat shows that this American Wirehair's hair tips are bent, producing a rough, springy texture.*

above: *The curled-back ears of the American Curl give it a unique look among cat breeds.*

left: *Careful breeding to combine Burmese shape with tabby coat pattern produced this Asian ticked tabby.*

well as from the breeding program that produced the other Asians.

Other Asians in the United Kingdom owe their origin to a mating between a Burmese and a Chinchilla in 1981, the resulting kittens being so attractive that their owner, Baroness Miranda von Kirchberg, decided to develop the "Burmilla." The original kittens were all black-shaded silver but, with regular matings back to Burmese to maintain the correct type and coat, other colors and patterns were produced, including selfs, smokes, and tabbies, as well as the semi-longhaired Tiffanie, giving a wide variety of Asian breeds. More recently, New Zealand breeders have developed the Mandalay, a Burmese-shaped cat in a range of colors, although it is not accepted in as many patterns as the Asians in the United Kingdom.

The earliest of these breeds was the Bombay, produced in 1958 in the United States from crosses between Burmese and black American Shorthairs and developed to resemble a black Burmese with golden eyes. Bombays have also been developed in Britain from half-Burmese mated back to Burmese for several generations, as

Asians

The Asian group of breeds are developed from crosses between Burmese and other breeds. Different breeding programs in various countries have resulted in cats with the shape of a Burmese, but a wide range of colors and patterns. They illustrate how, by means of a careful and selective breeding program, it is possible to introduce new colors and patterns into an existing breed to produce an entirely new range.

right: *This chocolate silver-shaded is typical of a Governing Council of the Cat Fancy Burmilla. The Burmilla recognized by the Fédération Internationale Féline is slightly more "Chinchilla" in type and usually has a lighter coat.*

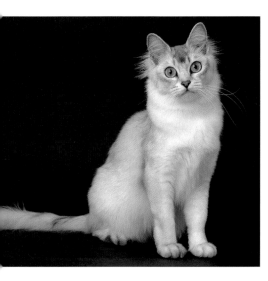

generation mated back to Burmese to achieve rich red cats of Burmese type that their breeder called "Carnelians." Unfortunately the breeder died before the Asians achieved popularity, but cats from her breeding line were able to join the Asian program.

Asian smokes, with their silver undercoats, are bred in the same colors as the selfs, plus these 13 colors in the Burmese version that lightens the color slightly, especially underneath the abdomen. (A brown Burmese is genetically a black cat lightened to brown by the Burmese gene.)

Burmillas and the Asian tabbies are produced in all 26 color schemes, but in addition they may or may not be silver. This means that each breed could be any one of 52 color combinations. Burmillas have a shaded or tipped coat pattern, with a pale undercoat and darker tips to the hair, while Asian tabbies are bred in spotted, classic, mackerel, and ticked patterns.

When it comes to the Tiffanie—the semi-longhaired Asian with its Burmese shape covered in a silky semi-long

The Asian selfs are bred in black (the Bombay), blue, chocolate, lilac, caramel, red, cream, and apricot, plus the five tortoiseshell colors: black, blue, chocolate, lilac, and caramel. The red selfs were bred for many generations before the other Asians, each

above: *The Bombay is a "Burmese in black patent leather."*

coat—there is a bewildering choice of 312 color schemes, since they may be bred in all the colors and patterns of the Asian Shorthairs, plus the 13 basic colors in their Burmese version!

Although they are some of the newest breeds to be recognized, the Asians have proved extremely popular. They have inherited the friendly, outgoing, talkative character of the Burmese, but usually without the extremes of character seen in some Burmese, making them ideal pets for someone who likes a cat to help with their activities. With their short, sleek coats, the Asian Shorthairs need minimal grooming, while the Tiffanies need little more, since their silky coats lack the thick undercoat of the Persian breeds.

left: *This brown Asian smoke shows a pure silver undercoat when the hair is parted.*

Bengal

Another of the more recent breeds, the Bengal was produced in the United States from matings between domestic cats and Asian Leopard Cats. The resulting kittens were so attractive that breeders worked to develop them into a new breed, with the wild appearance of their Leopard Cat ancestor combined with the temperament of a domestic cat.

It was not an easy breed to develop, since the males from the first cross (known as the F1 generation) are sterile, while the females are sub-fertile and produce few kittens. However, with matings to various domestic cat breeds, the fertility improved over the generations and Bengals became established.

Bengals are bred in two patterns, spotted and marbled, and in three intensities of color: brown, AOC-eyed snow, and blue-eyed snow. Some Bengals also carry the dilute gene, so blue cats are occasionally produced.

The Bengal coat should be very soft and velvety, quite unlike that of other cats. The marbled pattern consists of horizontal swirls of darker color down the body. The ideal spotted markings are those where the centers of the spots are paler, forming a ring of small spots known as a rosette. In brown Bengals the markings are black or brown on a background as rich as possible in color; the coat should have a glittering appearance when the light catches it. Blue-eyed snow Bengals have a Siamese coat pattern, with muted markings on the pale body shading to darker markings on the head, legs, and tail, while AOC-eyed snow Bengals have

Burmese or Tonkinese color distribution intermediate between the two.

Although early-generation Bengals tend to have the timid nature of their Asian Leopard Cat ancestors, later generations are friendly and playful, similar to a Burmese. They are large and very athletic, thinking nothing of jumping to the top of a door or leaping from the top of the drapes, and they love to play with water.

Birman

The first of the non-Persian longhaired breeds to be recognized, the Birman is a strong, muscular cat, with head and body longer that those of the Persian. It has a distinctive coat pattern: the basic color is that of the Siamese, with darker face, ears, legs, and tail contrasting with the pale body, but it must also have four white feet without white patches elsewhere. The front feet have neat white gloves covering the toes, while on the back feet the white extends up the back of the leg. Because of their Siamese color, all Birmans have blue eyes.

above: *Birmans are bred in many colors. This seal tortie point is one of the newer ones.*

right: *This brown spotted Bengal has a rich undercoat and should lose its few ticked hairs by the time it is mature.*

talkative, although less so than the Foreign and Oriental breeds, and make excellent pets. They seem to increase in popularity each year in Britain and are now seen in large numbers on the show bench up and down the country.

For many years, only seal point and blue point Birmans were recognized, but careful breeding programs, involving matings to other breeds, introduced other colors. Today Birmans are also bred in chocolate, lilac, red, and cream points, seal, blue, chocolate, and lilac tortie points, and all ten colors of tabby point—all with white feet. Although some registering bodies recognize all of these colors, others only accept the original seal and blue points.

Birmans are classed as semi-longhairs; their coats are long but the hair is silky and they lack the profuse undercoat of the Persian, so they do not need daily grooming throughout the year, although they need regular attention to prevent knots. They are generally livelier than Persians and rather more

British, European, and American Shorthairs

British Shorthairs have been developed from shorthaired non-pedigree domestic cats. A variety of shorthaired domestic breeds appeared at cat shows in the nineteenth century and formed the basis for the development of the British Shorthair as a distinct breed.

Similar developments took place elsewhere, with the American Shorthairs and European Shorthairs making the move from non-pedigree household pet classes to recognized breeds. They are rather less cobby and massive than the British, but are otherwise very similar. They are recognized in a variety of colors and patterns by different organizations.

British Shorthairs are powerful, cobby cats with rounded heads and bodies and a short, dense coat. They are bred in a wide variety of colors and patterns; most have orange eyes, although in the black silver tabbies they are green or hazel and the black-tipped and golden-tipped have green eyes.

The best known is the blue, but British Shorthairs are bred in many self colors—white (with blue, orange, or odd eyes—one blue, one orange), black, red, cream, chocolate, lilac, and, most recently, cinnamon and fawn. They are also bred in black, chocolate, lilac, and blue tortie, the latter known as blue-cream in this breed.

The tabbies are also well known, silver tabbies in particular having been popular from the earliest days of the breed. They are now bred in black, blue, chocolate, lilac, red, cream, and the four tortie colors and the silver versions of all of these, in spotted, classic, and mackerel patterns, although the mackerel is rarely seen. It is easy to see why the silver tabbies have been so popular, because a clearly marked silver tabby or spotty is a very striking cat.

right: *This attractive combination of silver tabby and white is not recognized by many registering organizations.*

below left: *The red and white bi-color has the cobbiness so typical of British Shorthairs.*

left: *The Colorpointed British Shorthair is bred in a wide range of points colors. These kittens were two of the earliest blue and blue tortie points to be bred.*

right: *The British blue, one of the original colors of the breed, is also the best known.*

Bi-color and tortoiseshell and white British, with their clear patches of color and white, are also very eye-catching. They are bred in black, blue, chocolate, lilac, red, and cream, but not yet in cinnamon or fawn. Tabby and white, tortie-tabby and white, and smoke and white are not recognized colors of British Shorthair, although they are acknowledged in some other domestic shorthair breeds.

British smokes, with their lovely contrasting silver undercoat that's only visible when their hair is parted are recognized in all British Shorthair colors except cinnamon and fawn. Although they have had full recognition for over 20 years, they are still uncommon.

British tipped, developed from crosses between British Shorthairs and Chinchillas, are bred in the usual color range, although the black tipped are by far the most common; their silver coats, lightly tipped with color, give a beautiful sparkling effect. The non-silver version of the black tipped is recognized as the golden tipped, the undercoat being a rich apricot color.

above: *The British tipped combines the delicate color of the Chinchilla with true British type.*

The Colorpointed British Shorthair has the color of a Siamese, with blue eyes but the sturdy cobby shape of the true British. The points color may be any of the recognized British colors, the cinnamon and fawn points being the most recently recognized. Unlike the other Siamese-colored breeds in Britain, there are also smoke points and silver tabby points, although not yet in cinnamon or fawn.

The British is a somewhat independent character, friendly but not demanding, with a fairly quiet voice. Although the coat is short it is very thick and requires regular grooming, especially when the cat is shedding.

above: *The Chartreux is a breed in its own right, although it is similar to a British blue or European Shorthair.*

Chartreux

Similar to a British blue, but slightly longer and less cobby, the Chartreux originated in France but is now widely recognized as a breed in its own right.

below: *The brilliant orange eyes of this British cream are set in a cream coat that should, ideally, show no tabby markings.*

Burmese, American Burmese

The Burmese is an elegant, muscular cat that should feel solid and heavy for its size. What started as a single breed on both sides of the Atlantic has diverged into two distinctly different ones.

The breed originated from one small brown cat—Wong Mau—who was imported from Myanmar (Burma) to the United States in 1930. She was mated to a Siamese and produced Siamese and brown kittens, but when the brown kittens were mated together, brown Burmese were produced and a new breed was born. From the results of the matings, it's likely that Wong Mau was a Tonkinese rather than a Burmese. Although the new breed was popular, it was some time before it was universally recognized in the United States, being accepted by the Cat Fanciers' Association in 1956.

A male and two females were imported into Britain in 1949, followed by a second male in 1953. This cat happened to carry the dilute gene, and a couple of years later when he was mated to one of his daughters, the first blue Burmese were born.

In the late 1960s and early 1970s, both chocolate and lilac Burmese were produced in Britain, some descended from the original imports and others from chocolate Burmese imported from the United States. At the same time, a breeding program in Britain set out to introduce the red gene into Burmese, producing, eventually, red, cream and brown, blue, chocolate, and lilac tortoiseshells. Although all of these colors are recognized by the British, the same is not true of all registering bodies in other countries.

The Burmese gene lightens the color slightly, especially on the underside, so a genetically black cat

below: *This row of Burmese kittens shows the American color range: lilac (platinum), chocolate (champagne), blue, and brown (sable).*

becomes brown. In some Burmese, especially chocolates, reds, and creams, the ears, face, and tail tend to be darker than the rest of the cat.

Burmese in Britain have changed remarkably little since they were first imported, although some have slightly shorter noses than those early imports. In the United States, however, some breeders selected to produce a much rounder-headed, shorter-nosed cat, quite distinct in shape from the original cat. Unfortunately, together with the new shape, some of these cats carried a gene that produced severe head malformations and many deformed kittens were produced.

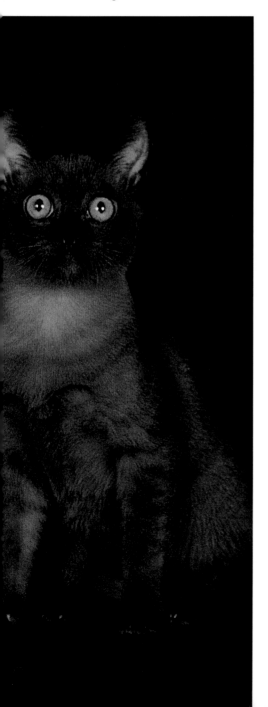

left: *The red Burmese is one of the newer colors and, like all red cats, shows slight tabby markings.*

For this reason, the Governing Council of the Cat Fancy will not allow imported Burmese to be registered, because they do not wish to risk introducing this gene into the British population.

Meanwhile in the United States, other breeders wished to perpetuate the original style of Burmese, so two distinct types of cat were recognized as the same breed, leading to a great deal of discussion about which was the correct type for the breed. This was eventually solved by keeping the name Burmese for the new style cat and renaming the traditional style cat "European Burmese."

Burmese are usually highly fertile cats and have been used to develop various other breeds in many different countries over the years: they have been mated to Siamese to produce Tonkinese worldwide and are the origin of the various Asian breeds—Bombays in the United States, Burmillas, other Asian Shorthairs, and Tiffanies in Britain, and Mandalays in New Zealand. Burmese were also one of the original breeds used in the development of the Australian Mist and the Bengal.

Burmese are very active, inquisitive, and talkative cats. They enjoy climbing and jumping, love attention, and can be very demanding, but they make excellent companions. Their short, sleek coats need minimal grooming, leaving more time for their owners to play with them.

Cornish Rex

The Cornish Rex originates, as its name suggests, in the county of Cornwall, England. In 1950 an ordinary tortoiseshell cat produced a litter that included a male kitten with a strange curly coat. The kitten, who was named Kallibunker, was mated to his mother, who then produced more curly kittens, proving that this strange coat was caused by a recessive mutant gene.

Only one of the curly kittens from this litter survived to maturity and he was later accidentally rendered sterile. By the time there was interest in perpetuating the new breed, there was only one curly-coated descendant of Kallibunker with which to start a breeding program. He was mated to Burmese and British Shorthairs to widen the gene pool and the breed became established.

above: *This red Cornish Rex is typical of the British standard for the breed.*

left: *The Cornish Rex has a neatly waved coat that shows beautifully on this tortie and white cat.*

Some of these early Cornish Rex were exported to the United States, where they were mated to Siamese and Orientals, thus producing a more fine-boned version of the breed. One of their descendants was imported back to Britain to widen the gene pool further.

The Cornish Rex is elegant but solid, with large, high-set ears and long legs and tail, but its distinctive feature is

below: *This elegant cat displays the more extreme type of Cornish Rex from the United States.*

the coat, which is curly or wavy all over the body—even the whiskers and eyebrows are curly. It may be any color or pattern, since this is not an important feature of the breed.

They are lively, affectionate cats and their coats require virtually no grooming, so they make excellent pets.

German Rex

In Germany, a curly-coated cat was found in 1949, but it was not until 1957, when she was mated to her straight-coated son, that further curly-coated kittens were produced. Some German Rexes were exported to the United States where matings to Cornish Rex produced curly kittens, proving that the two breeds were caused by the same gene mutation.

The German Rex, which is not very common, has a heavier build than the Cornish Rex and a rounder head.

Devon Rex

In 1960, in Buckfastleigh in Devon, England, a tortie-and-white ex-stray produced a litter of kittens that included one with a curly coat, just like the feral tom who had been seen in the neighborhood. Since the Cornish Rex had been discovered over the county border, it was assumed that this new curly coated cat was caused by the same gene, so he was mated to a Cornish Rex.

All the kittens were straight-coated, proving that this was a new recessive gene, but unfortunately some of the kittens were used for breeding, so there were many cats that carried both Rex genes and breeders had to work hard to separate the breeds again.

Devon Rexes have a unique look, with their large "jug-handle" ears and pixie faces. Their curly coats are often less neatly waved than the Cornish Rex and some suffer from very sparse coats with virtually bald bellies. Color is again unimportant, so Devon Rex may be any combination of colors and patterns.

Devons have very lively, inquisitive natures and make excellent pets.

Ohio Rex

In the early 1950s some Rex-coated kittens were produced by an ordinary domestic cat in Ohio, but no further breeding was done.

Oregon Rex

Further Rex kittens were produced in Oregon in 1964, again from a non-pedigree shorthaired cat. The hair quality suggested that this mutation was probably caused by the same gene as the Cornish Rex.

Ural Rex

Yet another Rex cat exists in Russia, where it has apparently been known for several decades. It is somewhat rounded in both head and body shape and the curly coat may be short or semi-long, although the semi-longhaired version is not very popular. Test-matings have shown that it is not caused by the same gene as the Cornish Rex, but it has not yet been test-mated to a Devon Rex.

left: *In the smoke Egyptian Mau the ghost tabby pattern must show very clearly.*

Egyptian Mau

This breed, which originated in Egypt, is a foreign-type spotted cat similar to the cats depicted in ancient Egyptian art. It must not be confused with the Oriental Spotted tabby, which, in its early days, was also called Egyptian Mau, although it has no connection with that country.

The breed was started in 1953 with cats from the Egyptian Embassy in Rome. In 1956 three Egyptian Maus from this line were imported into the United States. It is from these three cats that the breed was derived, although further cats have been imported since, to enlarge the gene pool and improve health and fertility.

right: *Silver Egyptian Maus have a very striking pattern of spots on a silver background.*

Several Egyptian Maus have recently been imported into Britain, where a group of breeders hope to develop the breed. They cannot compete at shows there, as the breed has not yet been recognized in that country, but they can be seen on exhibition at various shows.

The Mau is an elegant cat with a body similar to an Abyssinian, a modified wedge-shaped head, and a worried expression. It has a distinctive spotted pattern and comes in three main colors—bronze with black spots on a rich coppery brown background; silver with black spots on a silver background; and smoke, which, although genetically not a tabby cat, has very strong ghost tabby markings, producing black markings on a smoky silver background. Blue spotted, blue silver, and blue smoke Maus are also produced, although they are rarely seen and are not universally recognized. Self black and self blue cats are also sometimes produced, but cannot be shown. Egyptian Maus make lively and devoted pets.

Exotic Shorthair

The Exotic Shorthair is essentially a shorthaired Persian, with the identical cobby body, round head with a rather flattened face, sturdy legs, and short tail. There had been innumerable accidental matings between Persians and various shorthaired breeds over the decades, but eventually breeders set out to produce a cat with the appeal of the Persian but without its attendant grooming problems.

The breed was formally recognized in the United States in 1967, with the

left: *This chocolate Exotic Shorthair shows its Persian ancestry very clearly.*

in Persians (see pages 162–167), plus some additional colors and patterns, such as spotted and mackerel tabbies, blue pewter, and blue-shaded silver. With their big round eyes, they have an appealing look whatever their color.

The coat of the Exotic, although genetically shorthaired and far shorter than a Persian coat, is slightly longer

ingredient breeds restricted to Persians and American Shorthairs, although now only outcrossing to Persians is permitted. British breeders became interested and some cats were imported, while other breeders produced further Exotics from matings between Persians and British Shorthairs. The breed was eventually recognized in Britain in 1986. In order to protect the parent breeds, Exotic Shorthairs cannot be used for breeding British Shorthairs or Persians, the longhaired kittens that are sometimes produced being known as Exotic variants, not Persians.

Exotic Shorthairs are bred in the entire range of colors and patterns seen

than other shorthairs and very dense, making it stand out from the body of the cat. Being so thick, it needs regular grooming to keep it in good order, although it does not need the daily grooming essential for a Persian coat.

Exotic shorthairs are livelier than Persians, although much more sedate than the foreign breeds, and are generally well behaved. They make the ideal pet for someone who likes the Persian look and temperament but does not have time for daily grooming.

above: *Exotic Shorthairs are bred in all the Persian colors, plus some additional patterns.*

left: *This golden Exotic has all the appeal of a golden Persian, but without the daily grooming.*

feature is its tail. This is short, straight or bent, and usually carried upright, with the tail fur standing out like a pompom. This bobbed tail is often seen in domestic cats in the Far East.

The Japanese Bobtail Shorthair has a silky coat, long for a shorthaired cat but with no undercoat, while the Longhair has, as its name says, long hair, but still silky and without a thick undercoat, so although it needs regular grooming it does not need daily attention.

They are bred in a wide range of colors and patterns—selfs in black, blue, red, cream, or white, torties and blue torties, tabbies and bi- and tri-colors in all grades of white spotting, from more color than white, to the van pattern—white with a few colored spots. The traditional favorite color is white with patches of red and black, known as "Mi-ke" in this breed, but all colors and patterns are considered equal on the show bench.

Japanese Bobtails are friendly, intelligent, easygoing cats with quiet, musical voices, and they make good pets.

Japanese Bobtail

Despite its name, the Japanese Bobtail probably originated in China or Korea, but was taken to Japan centuries ago, possibly to kill mice. Although it was a farm or working cat, it can be seen in many examples of early Japanese art. The breed was imported into the United States in 1968 and soon gained recognition. In fact, at that time, more interest was shown in the breed in the United States than in its "native" Japan.

The Japanese Bobtail is a medium-sized cat, lean and muscular, with long legs and a somewhat triangular head, but its distinctive

Korat

The Korat is another naturally occurring breed, having been known in its native Thailand for many centuries, where it is described in the early *Cat Book Poems*, which present the "good luck" cats. In Thailand this blue cat is known as the Si-Sawat.

In 1959 the first Korats were imported into the United States, where the breed was developed without outcrosses to other breeds. It is possible that these were not the first Korats in the West, since the "all-blue Siamese" imported from Bangkok and shown in Britain at the end of the

parting a little along the spine as the cat moves. Each hair is blue, paler at the roots and getting darker up the hair, but with a silver tip, giving the coat an unusual shine.

Although Korats have not been mated to other breeds, in their native country the cats were undoubtedly less fussy, so a few of the imports carried recessive genes, accounting for the appearance of the occasional Siamese-colored kittens, sometimes known as Snow Cats, and the even rarer lilacs.

Korats are lively and friendly, making excellent companions. They can be very talkative and sound threatening, but rarely mean it. Their silky coat needs minimal grooming.

above: *The true blue Korat has been known in its native Thailand for centuries.*

nineteenth century may have been a Korat, but nothing more was heard of it, and although people were aware of these blue cats, none were imported.

From the United States, Korats were exported to many other countries, the first ones arriving in Britain in 1972. Further Korats were imported from the United States and direct from Thailand to increase the gene pool, since no outcrosses were permitted. The breed increased slowly in numbers and popularity but even today Korats are not very common.

The Korat is an elegant foreign-type cat with a heart-shaped face and large, luminous green eyes. Its coat is very silky and slightly long for a shorthair,

right: *Korats have luminous eyes that look too large for their heart-shaped faces.*

left: *This tabby and white Maine Coon looks just like its farm cat ancestors.*

right: *This rumpy Manx is distinguished by its total lack of tail.*

Maine Coon

Originally farm cats in the State of Maine and probably descended from longhaired cats who accompanied British sailors across the Atlantic, Maine Coons appeared at U.S. cat shows in the nineteenth century but were eclipsed by the imported Siamese and Persians. They were almost ignored until the 1950s, when a club was formed and began stimulating renewed interest in this native American breed. Maine Coons have been exported worldwide, arriving in Britain in 1983, but have retained their natural, rugged appearance, despite their ever-increasing numbers and popularity.

A large, muscular cat, the Maine Coon is long in the body, giving it a typical rectangular outline, with a very long tail. The head is strong, with a square muzzle and large ears. It has an undercoat and a long, glossy topcoat, which protects the cat well in its natural environment. The ears and paws are tufted, with feathery hair streaming from the ears and between the toes. Although the coat is said to be virtually self-maintaining, Maine Coons need regular grooming to eliminate knots—and to remove any twigs and burrs acquired on outdoor excursions.

Although to many people the brown tabby typifies the breed, Maine Coons are bred in a variety of colors and patterns—selfs, tabbies, smokes and shadeds, in black, blue, red, cream, tortie and blue-tortie, silver or standard, and with or without white in varying amounts. Color and pattern, however, are considered less important than the shape and size of the cat.

Maine Coons make ideal family pets, friendly and gentle despite their size, with quiet voices. Although happy house cats, they really enjoy outdoor exercise and a good hunting session.

right: *The Maine Coon is an impressive cat of a very impressive size.*

Manx

The Isle of Man (part of the British Isles) is famous for its tail-less cats and legends of their origin abound. One says that the Manx slipped late onto Noah's Ark as the door was shutting and left its tail behind, another that the tail-less cats jumped ashore from a sixteenth century Spanish shipwreck and made their way across the rocks to the Isle of Man, where they bred and founded the colony. As the gene that causes the Manx is dominant, one individual, introduced from elsewhere or produced by a natural mutation, could easily have been responsible for the entire colony, since there was no natural route for other cats to reach the island and enlarge the gene pool.

Manx have been known as a show breed since the nineteenth century and have been exported worldwide, although they are rarely seen in large numbers. The desirable show specimen is the "rumpy," with a dimple where its tail should be, but "stumpies," with short tails, and tailed Manx are also produced. Manx have only a single gene for tail-lessness; those embryos with two such genes do not survive. Manx may also suffer from spina bifida or sphincter

problems, so they are not the easiest variety of cat to breed.

In addition to being tail-less, the Manx must have a distinctive double coat, with a short, very thick undercoat and a slightly longer topcoat, requiring regular grooming. Color and pattern are, however, of no importance—they may be any of the British Shorthair colors and patterns except for colorpointed. Despite the problems experienced by breeders, Manx make good, companionable pets.

Cymric

Longhaired Manx occasionally occur, and in some countries (although not in Britain) they have been developed as a separate breed—the Cymric. Like a Manx in every way except for the coat length, the Cymric too has a thick double coat.

left: *Although this Manx shows a clear tabby*
pattern, this is less important than its coat quality
and shape.

157

left: *Norwegian Forest Cats are bred in a range of colors. Unfortunately, the white ones are sometimes deaf.*

Norwegian Forest Cat

Another native breed, the Norwegian Forest Cat came from the forests of Norway, as its name suggests. These longhaired cats were probably brought back by the Vikings from their trips to the Near East, having been taken on as ships' cats to deal with mice and rats. In Norse legend, a pair of white cats pulled the chariot of the goddess Freya.

For centuries Norwegian Forest Cats were semi-wild farm cats, relying on their hunting abilities, but in the 1930s they appeared at cat shows in Norway.

Their export was banned for many years, so it was not until the 1970s that they were recognized elsewhere, and since then they have been widely exported. They were first accepted as a breed in Britain in 1989, and although still not very numerous, they are a popular breed on the show bench.

A big, strong cat, with long legs and a very long tail, the Norwegian has a square outline. The head is triangular, with the ears set upright. The breed is slow to mature, sometimes not reaching full development until four years old.

In keeping with its rugged northern origins, the coat of the Norwegian Forest Cat is long and thick, with a wooly undercoat and glossy water-repellent topcoat, and requires regular grooming to keep it in order. Color and pattern are not important, and they may be black, blue, red, cream, tortie or blue tortie, silver or standard, in any pattern except colorpointed and with or without any amount of white.

The Norwegian is a friendly and active breed, making a good family pet. As its origins suggest, it enjoys excursions outdoors, hunting, and climbing.

above: *Norwegian Forest Cats have long bushy tails.*

left: *This tabby and white Norwegian Forest Cat shows off its thick weatherproof coat.*

above: *The Ocicat's beautiful clear spotted pattern is shown in this chocolate example.*

above: *The cinnamon Ocicat is the same color as the sorrel (red) Abyssinian.*

Ocicat

A fairly recent breed, Ocicats were first produced in the United States from crosses between Abyssinians and Siamese in the 1960s. The clear spotted pattern interested breeders, and the breed was developed to try to emulate the appearance of an Ocelot in a purely domestic cat, using Abyssinians, Siamese, and American Shorthairs.

Although Ocicats were recognized for registration in 1966, the breed took a considerable time to develop and it was not until 1987 that they were granted Championship status by the CFA. They're still not a numerous breed, although they have been exported to several countries, including Great Britain, where they were granted preliminary recognition in 1997. The Ocicat has a long, solid, muscular body and a modified wedge head with a square muzzle, and is one the larger and more substantial foreign breeds. The spotted pattern is the essential feature of the breed; each hair is banded with light and dark color, the spots forming where dark bands come together on the surface of the coat. On the sides of the cat the spots should form a pattern of large spots surrounded by a ring of spots, while the spots along the back are smaller. The face has stripes on the cheeks and an "M" shape on the forehead, the tail has dark rings and spots, and spots extend well down the legs.

With its Abyssinian ancestry, the Ocicat is bred in Abyssinian colors—black, chocolate, cinnamon, blue, lilac, and fawn, and in the silver versions of these colors, all with clear spots against the paler background color.

Despite its wild appearance, the Ocicat is a loyal and affectionate pet. It is a lively breed and very playful but, unlike its Siamese ancestors, it has a quiet voice.

left: *This silver Ocicat kitten does not yet show the clarity of pattern expected in an adult.*

Oriental Shorthair

Oriental Shorthairs are the full-colored relatives of the Siamese and were developed from the Siamese breed. They are Siamese in shape and all except the foreign white have green eyes.

In the early 1950s a sealpoint Siamese was mated to a Russian blue and the resulting black kittens were mated back to Siamese in an attempt to produce a self chocolate cat. At the same time, a mating between a seal point and a half-Siamese produced a chocolate kitten by sheer luck. These early cats were mated back to Siamese to develop the breed that is now known as the Havana. Since many of these cats carried the dilute gene, lilac cats were also produced, as well as blacks and blues.

Another group of breeders set out to produce a blue-eyed white Siamese-type cat by mating a Siamese out to a white shorthair then back to Siamese each generation until all of the kittens produced were Siamese or "Siamese in white overcoats." The foreign white, which is not mated to the other Orientals in order to ensure that it is a pure Siamese under its white coat, and thus avoid potential deafness problems, was granted Championship status in 1977.

Matings to red point Siamese introduced the red gene, producing red and cream selfs and the various tortoiseshell colors. Oriental torties are now bred in black, blue, chocolate, lilac, caramel, cinnamon, and fawn. Oriental selfs mated to tabby point Siamese produced Oriental tabbies, in spotted, classic, mackerel, and ticked patterns, each pattern gaining full status in turn as the cats increased in numbers and success on the show bench.

There were also matings to other breeds: a cross between a chocolate point Siamese and a Chinchilla introduced both the dilute modifier gene and the wide band gene, as well as the silver gene that led to silver tabbies, smokes, and shaded. The dilute modifier converts blue, lilac, and fawn to caramel, a brownish-gray color, and cream to apricot, a rich hot cream with

above: *This red Oriental ticked tabby is one of the newer patterns, similar to that of the Abyssinian.*

right: *The Oriental spotted tabby is bred in a wide range of colors. This cat is a chocolate spotty.*

a metallic sheen; the wide band gene was responsible for the Oriental shaded, an agouti cat in which the color is restricted to the ends of the hair. A mating between a sorrel Abyssinian and a sealpoint Siamese introduced the cinnamon gene into Orientals. Combined with the dilute gene, this produces the fawn, a delicate rosy mushroom color.

One by one the colors and patterns were recognized, until by June 1999 only the caramel self remained at the earliest stage of recognition, while all the other colors and patterns except the fawn self and the smokes have full Championship status.

Orientals do not just have the shape of the Siamese, they also have their temperament, being very lively, playful, vocal cats, and ideal pets if you do not insist on a tidy home. With their short, sleek coats they need virtually no grooming, apart from the regular stroking that they demand.

Oriental Longhair/Angora

The mating that introduced the cinnamon gene into Orientals also

above: *The Oriental black is pure Siamese mischief in a black overcoat.*

introduced the longhair gene, since the sorrel Abyssinian happened to carry it; this led to longhaired Orientals being produced in the early 1970s. The breed was named Angora and was developed by a few breeders, the gene pool being

enlarged by matings to Balinese and shorthaired Orientals. Similar matings in other countries produced the same breed, which is known as the Oriental Longhair in the United States and Javanese or Mandarin in Europe.

Identical in type and temperament to its shorthaired relative, the Angora is bred in all of the Oriental colors and patterns. Although longhaired, the coat is fine and silky and requires minimal grooming.

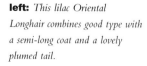

left: *This lilac Oriental Longhair combines good type with a semi-long coat and a lovely plumed tail.*

Persians

One of the best known and most numerous breeds, the Persian is descended from a mix of various longhaired breeds brought to Europe from the seventeenth century onward. Travelers to Turkey, Iran (then known as Persia), and Russia returned with much-prized longhaired cats.

A couple of centuries later, cat owners in Great Britain started to breed selectively for different colors and patterns, and by 1889 the Standard of Points drawn up by Harrison Weir specified the three groups into which longhaired cats were to be divided. Strangely enough, this was not by breed, the Persians, Russians, and Angoras all being included in each group, but by color: "White Long-haired Cat," "Black, Blue, Red, or Any Self Color Long-haired Cat," and "Brown, Blue, Silver, Light Gray, and White Tabby Long-haired Cats." As well as being judged together, the three breeds

right: *This red longhair shows its excellent type, despite being seasonally out of coat.*

were described as identical in shape, the only differences being the fine, silky coat of the Persian, the slightly wooly coat of the Angora, and the

left: *The cream longhair has beautiful copper eyes and a magnificent full coat.*

even woolier coat of the Russian. This seems strange, since today the coat of the Persian is usually more wooly than that of the Turkish Angora.

The Russians and Angoras faded from the scene and in a few years the Persian was the only longhaired breed worth mentioning. Blues and blue-eyed whites were particularly popular, and in addition to the colors described by Harrison Weir, torties, tortie and whites, smokes, and Chinchillas were also shown. Cat clubs were formed to cater to the various breeds, show classes were rearranged, and the tabby and white was removed from the tabby class and relegated to "Any Other Color," where it joined the other cats of no recognized breed.

The longhaired cats were sometimes called Persians, sometimes Longhairs. In 1910 the Governing Council of the Cat Fancy was organized; the clubs yielded power to this new body, and it was decreed that Persians would be

above: *Different registering organizations recognize different colors of Persian. This blue silver shaded is not yet recognized in Britain.*

below: *Blue-eyed whites were some of the earliest longhaired cats on the show bench.*

known as Longhairs, each color becoming a separate breed.

One by one, over the years, breeds progressed from the "Any Other Color" class, or from classes shared with other colors, to be dignified with classes of their own. The blue-creams did not achieve this until 1930,

although they had existed as a step in the breeding of creams since the very early days. The bi-colors, present from the start, waited until the 1960s for their own class, and the tabby bi-colors, removed from the tabby class decades before, did not appear for another 20 years.

Not content with perfecting existing breeds, some breeders set out to produce something new. In the 1950s a group worked to introduce the Siamese coat pattern into the Longhairs without losing the true Persian type and coat. Their careful breeding program was successful and colorpoints were accepted in seal, blue, chocolate, and lilac point versions. Further work led to the recognition of red points and seal tortie points, followed by the other three tortie point colors and the cream point. Eventually, in the early 1980s, tabby points in all ten colors were accepted.

left: *Tortoiseshell longhairs have been shown from the very early days onward. Their coats must show clear red and black colors.*

above: *A show quality brown tabby is very difficult to achieve. Not only must the coat and type be right, the tabby pattern has to be distinct.*

More new breeds were to follow: the chocolate gene had been introduced into the Longhairs when the colorpoints were produced and it was now spread further through the section to give chocolate selfs, torties, tortie and whites, bi-colors, tabbies, and smokes, together with its dilute, the lilac, in the same patterns.

The red gene was combined with the Chinchilla pattern to produce the red, cream, tortie and blue-cream cameos, with deep orange eyes instead of the emerald eyes of the Chinchilla. From these the pewter, an orange-eyed black silver shaded cat, was produced.

The shaded silver, a more heavily marked variety of the Chinchilla, was recognized as a separate breed and, to the breeders' surprise, the first golden Persians were produced from respectable Chinchilla lines, many of which were descended from recent American imports. The golden lacks

the gene for silver and has a rich apricot undercoat with dark tipped hairs, but with the same emerald eyes as its Chinchilla parents.

Meanwhile, in the United States, the longhaired cats had proved equally popular. They were known as Persians and each color was considered a variety rather than a separate breed. New color varieties were produced by the combination of various existing colors and patterns; an even wider range of colors and patterns is accepted by many of the registering bodies.

However, when Persians were mated out to Siamese to produce the Siamese-patterned Persian, the result was called a Himalayan, rather than

left: *Smoke longhairs have silvery white undercoats beneath a darker topcoat that may be black, blue, chocolate, lilac, red, cream, or tortie.*

many cases, contravenes the Standard of Points. There are therefore two different types of Persian Longhair competing against each other on the show bench'.

Unfortunately, the breeding to produce a shorter and shorter cat introduced various health problems over the decades: many of the jaws became narrow, undershot or twisted, with teeth at very strange angles, sometimes sticking out sideward. The very flat-faced cats are often overshot kittens, sometimes to a marked degree. Instead of being rounded, the skulls developed bumps and grooves, and the noses were distorted with narrowed or sometimes almost nonexistent nostrils, making it difficult for the cats to breathe. In addition to this, the skin folds on the face sometimes rubbed on the surface of the eye, producing permanent irritation.

In Britain, a list of defects was added to the Standard of Points booklet, drawing attention to various anatomical abnormalities that prelude a cat from winning high awards. This had some effect and far fewer cats with severe abnormalities are now seen on the show bench.

Persians are not particularly lively or talkative cats so they make very good pets for people who want a well-behaved and undemanding cat, but they need much more care and attention than any other breed. Many suffer from watery eyes because their tear ducts are inadequate, and need their faces wiped to prevent staining of the hair and excoriation of the skin. Those with maloccluded teeth need their mouths checked regularly to

being considered as another variety of Persian, although the shape was identical.

Longhaired cats at the turn of the century looked very little like those of today: they were rangier in the body and had longer noses and bigger ears, and could easily be mistaken for Maine Coons. Over the decades the breed changed: the body became cobbier, the tail shorter, and the head rounder, with neat small ears and big round eyes. The coat became more profuse, with more undercoat, so that grooming became more and more of a full-time job.

As with so many breeds, the Persian changed more in the United States than in Britain. Whereas in Britain many breeders prefer an open face, with a short neat nose whose nose leather does not go higher than the lower eyelid, in the United States the face has been flattened further and the nose is often placed between the eyes. Some British breeders have followed this lead and, either by importing cats or selecting from their own stock, have produced a similar type of cat that, in

left: *This red point colorpoint (Himalayan) has impressive type but is very short of coat after a long, hot summer.*

above: Silver tabbies look magnificent, but it is very difficult to achieve a clear pattern.

make sure that there are no teeth rubbing on the lips or palate. But most time-consuming of all, Persians need daily grooming to prevent their coats from matting and to keep them in good order. Anyone who lacks the time for frequent grooming should not even consider owning a Persian cat.

above: Black Persians have dense black coats as adults, but kittens often have gray undercoats.

right: This golden Persian kitten will take a while to develop the beautiful apricot coat color of the adult.

Selkirk Rex

In 1987 in Wyoming, a normal female cat produced a curly-haired kitten after mating with an unknown tom. This kitten was mated to a black Persian and produced a mixed litter of curly-coated and normal kittens, thus proving that this was a new and dominant Rex gene, since only a single gene was required to produce the Rex coat. A selective breeding program produced the Selkirk Rex, which is now recognized by several registering bodies in the United States and Europe, although not in Britain. It still has only provisional recognition with the Cat Fanciers' Association and is not yet recognized by the Fédération Internationale Féline.

A medium to large cat, with a cobby body and rounded head, the Selkirk is similar in type to the British Shorthair,

left: Clear tabby markings on the head, legs, and tail distinguish this chocolate tabby point Siamese.

which is one of the breeds to which it may be outcrossed. Persians and Exotics may also be used in the CFA breeding program at present and American Shorthairs were permitted until January 1, 1998.

The coat of the Selkirk Rex is dense, plush, and curly, with random curls rather than neat waves, giving an untidy look. It may be either shorthaired or longhaired, the difference being more clearly visible on the tail and around the neck, where the curls of the longhaired variety stand out, looking even less tidy than the shorthaired variety.

The Selkirk Rex is bred in most colors and patterns, including selfs, torties, tabbies, shaded and tipped, bi- and tri-colors, and Siamese, Burmese, and Tonkinese colors.

With its background of Persian, Exotic, and British breeding, the Selkirk Rex is very different from the other Rex breeds. It has a less adventurous nature, but it makes a good pet for someone with a taste for unusual-looking cats.

Siamese

The Siamese is one of the best known breeds and also one of the oldest. Like the Korat, it appears in the *Cat Book Poems*, which are thought to date from the sixteenth century. Siamese became royal pets in Thailand and could not be owned by commoners.

In 1885 two "Royal Cats of Siam" appeared at a cat show in London, having been given to the outgoing

above: This young seal point Siamese will darken as it matures, but should always show good contrast between the body and point colors.

British Consul by the King of Siam. Further cats were imported and by the turn of the century the breed was well established.

Although black, chocolate, and bluepoint cats were registered as Siamese in the early days, the seal point was regarded as the only desirable color and the blue point was not recognized until 1936. This was followed by the chocolate point in 1960 and the lilac point in 1970. Although some lilac points were bred from existing Siamese lines, others descended from outcrosses to the Russian Blue that produced the early Orientals. This Russian Blue therefore appears far back in the pedigrees of many so-called "pure" Siamese.

Red point Siamese had been seen in the 1930s but the first officially recognized one in Britain was born in 1948 from a tortie half-Siamese mated to a Siamese stud. Despite the efforts of the breeders to get them recognized as Siamese, red and tortie points remained as "Any Other Variety Shorthairs" until 1966 when they, and the newer tabby points descended from tabby half-Siamese, were eventually recognized as Siamese.

They were joined by blue, chocolate, and lilac tortie points, then by red, cream, and tortie tabby points, then cream points, the latter gaining Championship status in 1977. No more Siamese colors were recognized until, in 1994, cinnamon, caramel, and fawn points and their tortie, tabby, and tortie-tabby versions were given preliminary recognition. Finally, in 1998, they were joined by the apricot points and apricot tabby points.

Not all of these colors are recognized in other countries, and indeed, the CFA in the United States recognizes only the seal, blue, chocolate, and lilac points as Siamese, the red, tortie, cream, and tabby points being considered colorpoint shorthairs.

The Siamese is a medium-sized, long, elegant cat, with long legs and tail, a triangular-shaped head, and large ears that follow the lines of this triangle. The Siamese gene restricts the darker color to the face, ears, legs, and tail, contrasting with the paler body color. The eyes, of course, are always blue.

Siamese are very playful, active cats with loud, demanding voices. They are also thieves and are very good at

above: *Although this cream point Siamese was born in the 1970s, the breed has not changed since.*

hiding small objects such as pens, teaspoons, and jewelry if their owner is unwise enough to leave them lying around. If you enjoy a life without a dull moment, get a Siamese.

Balinese

Balinese are essentially semi-longhaired Siamese, are bred in the same range of colors, with the exception of the cinnamon and fawn series, and have the same personality. The breed originated in the United States in the late 1960s, although there had been an attempt to get them recognized in the 1940s. The first Balinese were bred in

Britain in 1974 from imported cats, but there was a brief delay before other cats were imported and the breed became popular.

The CFA recognizes only the seal, blue, chocolate, and lilac points as Balinese. The other colors are known as Javanese—not to be confused with the European Javanese, which are Oriental Longhairs.

Balinese are bred back to Siamese regularly to enlarge the gene pool. The resulting shorthaired kittens are known as Balinese variants and are used for breeding Balinese only, although some registering bodies permit these cats to be shown as Siamese.

below: *This tortie point Balinese clearly shows her Siamese ancestry.*

above: *In tortie points any shading on the body is slightly mottled. This champion chocolate tortie point shows excellent contrast.*

above: *This Siberian cat has the most superb set of whiskeres, as well as a good, thick coat.*

Siberian

This breed is similar to the Maine Coon or Norwegian Forest Cat in appearance, nature, and origin, being a large, rugged semi-longhaired cat that originated, in this case, in the Russian forests.

The breed has probably existed for many centuries, although it is only fairly recently that it has been shown, even in Russia. The cats were never seen outside Russia, probably due to the difficulties in traveling in and out of Russia and further difficulties transferring money. In 1987, however, two cats were exported to Berlin and the breed started to become established outside its native country, spreading around Europe and to the United States. The spread of the breed was probably aided by the more relaxed political situation and the fact that people travel long distances across Europe to show in different countries.

right: *Siberian cats have now spread worldwide from their Siberian forests.*

It is now fairly well recognized as a distinct breed, although not by the CFA or in Britain.

The Siberian is a big, strong cat, rounder in shape than the other two forest breeds. The body is long and rounded, the feet are big and rounded, and the head is a rounded modified wedge, with medium-sized

above: *The particularly heavy ruff of fur around the neck helps to keep the cat warm in the Siberian winter.*

ears. The coat is semi-long to long, with a very thick undercoat, especially in winter, and a pronounced ruff protects the cat from

its harsh natural environment.

Although the brown tabby is probably the most typical pattern in the Siberian's native habitat, it is recognized in a variety of colors and patterns, color being a less important feature than shape or coat.

An active cat that loves to leap, the Siberian needs outdoor exercise to enjoy as natural a lifestyle as possible.

Singapura

The Singapura was originally a Singapore street cat, living in the drains and alleyways, but in 1975 three were imported to the United States, where the breed was developed. They were recognized by the CFA in 1982 and granted Championship status in 1988. Their importance has now been recognized in their home country, where they are the national mascot.

Although some Singapuras were imported to Britain in the late 1980s and were seen on exhibition at shows in 1989, they aroused little interest and it was another four years before a breed club was formed and Singapuras reappeared on exhibition. Further cats were imported to establish a sound gene pool, since Singapuras may not be mated to any other breed. A breeding program was started and in

1997 Singapuras were granted preliminary recognition and could compete at shows. Singapuras are now recognized by many, but not all, registering bodies worldwide.

Singapuras are medium-sized cats with a stocky build. The head is rounded with a medium-length muzzle and noticeably large eyes and

above: *The Singapura is an alert and very playful cat.*

ears. Their coats are very short and close-lying, requiring virtually no grooming, and they come in just one color and pattern. They are a golden ivory color, with the hairs on the body banded with sepia. They show some sepia striping on the face and minimal striping on the legs. Genetically, this color is produced by a combination of the Burmese gene and the ticked tabby pattern, with selection for the desired tone. The breed was mimicked by descendants of matings between Burmese and Abyssinians, but these are not accepted as true Singapuras.

Singapuras are very playful cats, joining in with family life in a big way, and make ideal pets. If ignored they demand attention, quietly and persistently.

left: *With its extra-large eyes and ears and delicate coloring, the Singapura is very distinctive.*

carried the longhair gene, so longhaired kittens were occasionally produced, but nobody thought of these as anything other than pets until the 1960s. Breeders in the United States decided to develop these longhairs as a distinct breed. In 1980 a group of breeders pooled resources to import a group of cats and start a breeding program in Britain, and Somalis were recognized as a breed two years later.

The Somali is an elegant, muscular cat of medium size, with a moderate, gently contoured wedge head. The coat is semi-long, soft and dense, lying flat over the shoulders and along the back, but with a ruff around the neck and breeches on the hind legs. Somalis need regular but not daily grooming.

It is essential for the coat to show ticking, with many color bands on each hair, but the ticking takes some time to develop fully and is not obvious on kittens. The original colors were the usual or ruddy, with a deep

Snowshoe

Developed in the United States in the 1960s, the Snowshoe resulted from crossing Siamese with bi-color American Shorthairs. The breed was slow to be accepted and is still not recognized by all U.S. registering bodies.

Snowshoes have been bred in Europe, using similar matings, but there, too, it is not universally acceptable as a distinct breed. In Britain the GCCF does not recognize it as a breed, but it may be shown at FIFe shows as an "unrecognized breed."

The Snowshoe is a medium to large muscular cat, which inherits the long body of the Siamese combined with the solidity of the American Shorthair. Its head is triangular, with large ears. The color is again a combination of its two parent breeds—the white markings of the bi-color combined with the color distribution of the Siamese. In keeping with this Siamese color, the Snowshoe has blue eyes. The short glossy coat requires little grooming.

Originally bred as seal points, which are still the most commonly seen color, Snowshoes are now recognized by The International Cat Association in seal, blue, chocolate, lilac, cinnamon, and fawn points, and in both mitted and bi-color patterns. Both patterns have white feet, but the

mitted is not more than one-third white and the bi-color may be up to two-thirds white and must have an inverted white "V" on the nose. Elsewhere there have been attempts to breed tortie and tabby point Snowshoes.

Although the Snowshoe is not universally recognized for showing, its attractive coloring makes it a very popular pet wherever it is found. It is a lively, friendly cat and very good company.

Somali

The Somali is essentially a longhaired Abyssinian. Several Abyssinian breeding lines on both sides of the Atlantic

rich orange undercoat and black ticking, and sorrel, with an apricot undercoat and cinnamon ticking, but Somalis are now also bred in blue, chocolate, lilac, fawn, red, cream, six tortie colors, and silver versions of all of these. All colors of Somali now have Championship status in Britain, but many of them, especially the red, cream, and tortie colors, are not recognized elsewhere in the world.

Somalis are lively, playful cats, affectionate with their owners but sometimes a little standoffish with strangers. They love outdoor exercise, leaping through vegetation with their tails held high.

Sphynx

Hairless cats have been produced in various countries at different times, but were not developed as a breed. However, in Canada in 1966 a hairless kitten was born in a litter of normal kittens and was kept for breeding, thus starting the Sphynx breed. It is recognized in Canada and by some organizations in the United States and Europe, but with many it is either at

an early stage of recognition or not recognized at all. Sphynx are produced by a recessive gene, requiring one gene from each parent. Although described as hairless, they do have a slight fuzzy "peach bloom," often with some hair on the feet, face, and the end of the tail. Their skin is wrinkled, although excessive wrinkling is undesirable.

They are medium to long cats with heavy bodies, wedge-shaped heads, and very large ears. They are bred in a variety of colors and patterns, these showing as skin pigment, since there is virtually no hair to be colored.

Although there is no coat to groom, some Sphynx suffer from greasy skin and have to be bathed. With no coat to protect them they must not get too cold and need protection from the sun to avoid sunburn and skin cancer, particularly in the lighter-colored varieties. They need owners who are prepared to give them this additional care. Sphynx are lively, playful cats who make good pets in the right homes.

Don Sphynx, Don Hairless

A very similar cat to the Sphynx but with a slightly heavier build was found in Russia in 1987 and proved to be a distinct breed caused by a dominant gene.

Peterbald

Produced in St. Petersburg from matings between Don Hairless and Orientals, the Peterbald is a hairless cat of Oriental type. Some have been exported to the United States.

below: *The Sphynx breed has a variable amount of hair on the head, legs, and tail, but just peach fuzz on the body, so all the wrinkles show.*

Tonkinese

The Tonkinese is essentially a cross between Burmese and Siamese. Many have been produced since Burmese were introduced to the West, and were probably first produced in the Far East, where both coat patterns exist. It is likely that Wong Mau, the founder of the Burmese breed, was actually a Tonkinese. However, it was not until 1965 in Canada that it was accepted as a distinct breed.

Even now, Tonkinese are fully recognized by relatively few registering bodies, due to their inability to breed true. They must have one Burmese and one Siamese gene, so two Tonkinese mated together produce Siamese and Burmese-patterned cats, as well as true Tonkinese.

right: *In Tonkinese the color shades gently from the darker points to the lighter body.*

The Tonkinese is midway between its parent breeds in both shape and color. In the United States, where many Siamese have been bred for extreme length and Burmese for shortness of head, there is room for an intermediate breed. In Britain, with more substantial Siamese and less

extreme Burmese, the gap between the two is not great, making it more difficult for the Tonkinese to be a distinct breed.

The coat pattern of the Tonkinese is a paler body shading gradually into a darker face, ears, legs, and tail, without the sharp distinction of color seen in the Siamese or the more even color of the Burmese. In the United States this pattern is known as Mink. The eyes are blue-green in color.

Tonkinese are bred in Britian in brown, blue, chocolate, lilac, caramel, red, cream, and apricot, the six tortie colors, and all 14 tabby colors. The recognized colors vary from country to country and some registering bodies accept the Siamese and Burmese patterned cats for competition as well as the Tonkinese or mink color.

Tonkinese are lively, playful cats and make excellent companions.

Turkish Angora

The Turkish Angora arrived in Europe in the seventeenth century and helped create the Persian. However, the popularity of the Persian overshadowed the Angora and the breed virtually died out except in its native Turkey. Although Angoras were mentioned during the nineteenth century, by the early twentieth century doubt was expressed that they really were a distinct breed and certainly it is hard to recognize them from their Standard of Points of the time.

A breeding program was set up at Ankara Zoo in the 1960s in order to maintain the breed. Some cats bred at the zoo were exported to the United States and a few to Europe. The very few that came to Britain were not maintained as a separate breed; the Turkish Angora is still not recognized by the GCCF today.

Turkish Angoras are medium to small in size, long-bodied but with high-set ears. They are quite unlike the Persian breed to which they contributed. Their coat is semi-long,

above: *This lilac Tonkinese shows the typical "midway between Siamese and Burmese" look.*

fine, and silky, with no undercoat, and needs only moderate grooming.

The traditional color in Turkey is the odd-eyed white, and the first color accepted was white, but Turkish Angoras are now bred in a wide range of colors and patterns, including all the self colors, torties, and tabbies.

In the United States, Turkish Angoras may not be mated to any other breed, but some European registering bodies allow crosses between Turkish Angoras and Turkish Vans to be registered as Turkish Angoras. They are not related in any way to the Angora recognized in Britain, which is an Oriental Longhair.

Turkish Angoras are playful but not noisy, and make lively companions.

Turkish Van

Another native breed, the Turkish Van was first imported from the Lake Van area of Turkey into Britain in 1955, with more cats following a few years later. The breed then developed slowly—with a limited gene pool, careful matings were essential—but in 1969 they were given Championship status as Turkish cats, their name later being changed to Turkish Van to indicate their distinctive coat pattern and to distinguish them from the Turkish Angora.

The Turkish Van is a large,

long-bodied, substantial cat, with a strong wedge-shaped head and sturdy legs. The coat is long and silky in the winter but shorter in the summer, with no undercoat, requiring only moderate grooming.

The distinctive pattern of this breed consists of a chalky white coat with a colored tail and two colored spots on the top of the head, at the base of the ears. A small colored spot or two on the body is not heavily penalized,

although they are not desirable. The original color of these cats was white with auburn markings and amber eyes, but blue-eyed and odd-eyed cats cropped up now and then, and although they could not be shown they were used in the breeding program.

At least one of the imported cats must have carried the dilute gene, since after a number of years cats with cream markings were born from legitimate Turkish Van breeding lines. The blue- and odd-eyed cats and the creams were given recognition by the GCCF and now both colors in all three eye colors have Championship status. In Europe black, tortie, and tabby marked Turkish Vans had been bred from different imported cats and some of these were imported into Britain, where breeders are working to gain recognition for them.

The Turkish Van is a strong and somewhat willful cat that enjoys swimming and playing with water. It makes a good pet and a superb show cat. A Turkish Van neuter, Supreme British Grand Premier Akdamar Bazisey Mahsus, is the only cat to have been awarded Supreme Exhibit at the GCCF Supreme Show for two years in succession.

below: *The Turkish Van has a chalk-white coat with clear patches of color on the head and a colored tail.*

lesser known breeds

American Bobtail

When a short-tailed kitten was found in Arizona in the 1960s, it mated with the family's pet Siamese and produced more short-tailed kittens. Further matings developed the breed and the American Bobtail was born.

It is a fairly large, substantial cat, with a broad wedge head and a short tail that may be straight or kinked. The coat is dense and may be long or short, and of any color or pattern.

The breed is not very common, even in its country of origin, so is unlikely to be found outside the United States.

Australian Mist

A breeding program was started in 1976 in Australia to develop a spotted cat of delicate coloration and moderate type. Half of the cats selected for the breeding program were Burmese, a quarter were Abyssinian, and a quarter domestic tabbies. After a decade of careful breeding, the Spotter Mist, now renamed the Australian Mist, was produced.

The breed is medium sized with a moderate rounded shape, rounded head, large ears, and large green eyes. They have short resilient coats in a delicate-colored spotted pattern, the muted color produced by the Burmese gene. The spots may be warm brown, blue, chocolate, lilac, gold, or peach against a misty ground; the legs and tail are ringed and barred and there are tabby lines on the face.

This is Australia's first home-produced new breed, but it has not yet been accepted elsewhere.

California Spangled Cat

In the 1970s, a breeder impressed by the wild leopards of Tanzania set out to breed a miniature domestic version. Eight different breeds, including Siamese and Abyssinians, contributed their qualities to the new breed.

The California Spangled Cat is long, lean, and muscular, and tends to walk with its body low to the ground, like a stalking leopard. The head is broad, with a full muzzle and prominent whisker pads. The coat is short and close, but slightly longer on the belly and tail, and is covered with clear spots that may be any of nine different colors. The preferred eye color is brown, to complement the coat.

Ceylon

Originating in Ceylon (now called Sri Lanka) and rarely seen, this breed is similar to the Singapura. Small to medium in size, the body is compact and muscular, and the head has rounded cheeks, a short nose, and a well-developed chin, with fairly large ears and large luminous eyes.

The coat is short and fine. The only permitted pattern is ticked tabby, which, unlike the Singapura, may be black, blue, red, cream, or tortie against a gold or sandy background.

Chausie

The Chausie is a fairly new breed, developed in the United States from a cross between the Jungle Cat (*Felis chaus*) and domestic cats of various different breeds, including Abyssinians and Bengals. They are therefore somewhat variable in appearance.

They are active, playful cats, and, like Bengals, enjoy playing with water.

Havana Brown

When Havanas were first developed in Britain in the 1950s, some cats were exported to the United States and founded the Havana Brown breed. Whereas in Britain Havanas were mated back to Siamese and the type

right: *This California Spangled kitten does not yet show the clarity of spotting that adults have.*

left: *The Havana Brown, an American breed, has moderate foreign type and green eyes.*

Karelian Bobtails may be any color combination, except for the Siamese or Abyssinian patterns.

Kurilian

Also originating from Russia and rarely seen, the Kurilian or Kuril Bobtail appears to be the same breed, although one is described as having a short tail, while the other has a tail of normal length.

The body is medium in size, sturdy and compact, while the head is triangular. The coat may be short or semi-long and all colors are accepted, apart from the Siamese or Abyssinian patterns or a solid white cat.

LaPerm

Developed from a female cat with curly coat found in Oregon, the LaPerm is a new breed that is still being developed. The curly coat, unlike that of the Cornish and Devon Rex, is caused by a dominant gene. LaPerms are quite rare in the United States and are not yet seen elsewhere.

The cat is medium in size, with an elegant, muscular body, medium-length legs, and tapered tail. The head is a broad wedge with rounded contours and the ears are slightly flared. The coat may be short and wavy or semi-long and distinctly curly but, at least once in its life, a LaPerm sheds its entire coat, the hair growing back even curlier than before.

Munchkin

Cats with very short legs were seen in Britain in the 1940s and in Russia in the 1950s, but they are now being developed as a breed in the United States. All the present representatives of the breed are descended from a black cat from Louisiana who possessed this naturally occurring mutated gene.

The shortened legs are caused by a dominant gene, so Munchkins mated to normal cats produce further Munchkins. The head, body, and tail are similar to a normal domestic shorthair, this being the permitted outcross breed, but the legs are distinctly shorter than normal and slightly bowed, although severely

improved over the generations, in the United States the original, stockier type was maintained, so that today the two are very different breeds, although they have the same origins, and are rarely seen outside the United States.

The Havana Brown is a medium-sized cat with a sturdy but not cobby body, long legs, and a medium-length tail. The head is fairly long, with a square muzzle and a definite stop in the profile. The coat is short and smooth. The Havana Brown is only recognized in chocolate and lilac colors.

Karelian Bobtail

This Russian breed is uncommon, although it has been recognized in its homeland since 1992. It is not a large breed, the body being elegant but muscular and the head triangular with large ears. The tail is 1.5–5.1 inches (4–13 cm) long, and the shiny topcoat forms a pompom on it. There is also a semi-longhaired variety in which the coat is medium in length, with a ruff at the neck.

right: *The curly coat of the unusual LaPerm may give the cat an untidy appearance.*

bowed legs are undesirable. The coat may be short or semi-long, again like that of a domestic shorthair, and may be any color.

The short legs are said not to inconvenience the cat, but most registering bodies will not accept the breed, regarding its deformity as undesirable.

Nebelung

Developed in the United States from a cross between blue domestic longhairs and Russian Blues, the Nebelung is one of the newer breeds and is not recognized by many organizations. Although some are said to have been imported into Britain, they have never appeared on exhibition.

An elegant cat with an angular, modified wedge head, the Nebelung resembles its American-style Russian

Blue ancestors. The coat is semi-long and silky, with a dense undercoat that makes it stand out from the body. The color is blue, with lighter shades preferred, and the hairs are silver tipped, giving a lustrous look.

Ojos Azules

All the cats of this interesting breed are descended from Cornflower, a tortoiseshell cat with blue eyes who was found in New Mexico in 1984. The blue eye color was caused by a dominant gene mutation, so the beautiful deep blue eyes were passed on to her kittens. Despite this, the

breed is still rare and being developed.

Generally only cats with the dominant white gene, the Siamese gene, or high grade white spotting have blue eyes, so this new mutation has caused a great deal of interest.

Pixie-Bob

The Pixie-Bob was developed in the United States with the idea of producing a domestic breed resembling the North American Bobcat. The cat is medium to large and somewhat rangy, with long, heavy-boned legs and large feet; polydactyls with five to seven toes are accepted in this breed. The tail is short and may be kinked, although this is less desirable. The head is an inverted pear shape with prominent brows, resembling that of the Bobcat.

The coat may be short, wooly, and resilient, or semi-long and silky. The pattern is brown spotted tabby, with or without rosettes, muted by heavy

left This shorthaired Munchkin obviously had some Siamese in its ancestry.

ticking, with a warm-toned background color. Each hair must be banded or the desired muted effect is not achieved.

Although the cat has been bred to look like a Bobcat, it is a purely domestic cat with a gentle temperament.

Sokoke

This breed comes from the Sokoke forest of southeast Kenya, where it is said to be nearing extinction. When a litter of Sokokes was found on a farm, some were sent to Denmark, since there were doubts that they would survive in their homeland, and a careful breeding program was followed. There are about 25 known breeding cats, in Italy, Holland, and Denmark and now the United States, too.

The Sokoke is a moderate-sized cat with an elegant, muscular body, high on the legs, a small head, and a long, slender tail. The coat is very short and shiny, with no undercoat. Only the marbled pattern is seen now, although spotted Sokokes had been seen in the past. The original cats were brown, but more recently a few blue-eyed snows have been born.

Tiffany/Chantilly

This breed, variously known as Tiffany, Chantilly, or Chantilly/Tiffany, has a somewhat mysterious origin. It started in 1967 with two chocolate semi-longhaired cats of unknown background who were being sold as part of an estate sale. The suggestion that these cats had a Burmese origin persisted for many years, although they showed no sign of the Burmese gene. The breed is very rare and recognized by few registering bodies.

It is a semi-foreign medium-sized cat with semi-foreign body and head type. Its full semi-long coat flows and its tail is a magnificent plume. The best-known color is chocolate, but they are also bred in blue, cinnamon, lilac, and fawn, in both self and tabby patterns, all with golden eyes.

Traditional Siamese/Thai

Breeders in several countries have worked to recreate a breed similar to very old-fashioned pet type Siamese, with cobbier bodies and rounder heads than the true Siamese has had for many decades. This breed, which is not widely recognized, is variously known as the Traditional Siamese or the Thai.

York Chocolate

The York Chocolate breed is descended from a self chocolate semi-longhaired kitten who was born in 1983 in New York state. The parents were both black semi-longhaired farm cats who presumably had some Siamese blood in their ancestry.

The body is medium to large with head, legs, and tail in proportion. The coat is semi-long, smooth, and glossy, with no undercoat. The color is a rich chocolate or lilac, with or without white, and the eyes are green, gold, or hazel.

The breed is not numerous and is recognized by very few organizations.

below: *The York Chocolate, a very uncommon breed, may have any amount of white spotting on its chocolate coat.*

showing

If you want to show your cat you should visit a show first to see what is involved. At most shows the cat remains in its pen all day, being removed and examined by each judge in turn. You may have to buy a white blanket, white litter box, and white water and food bowls for it, so that the cat is identified only by its number.

At most other shows the cat spends the day in a pen that may be decorated and is taken to a plain pen for judging; you therefore need to find out the size of the pen and make drapes to decorate it, as well as supply a litter box, food and water bowls, etc. You can usually buy all the white equipment from stands at shows.

Pen your cat at home sometimes so that the restriction does not come as a surprise. Get it used to its traveling box as well: a top-opening box or basket is the most practical, unless you can guarantee that the cat will walk out happily, since dragging out a reluctant cat is not the best start to the day and may ruin a longhair's grooming.

Make sure that your cat is suitable for showing. Shows put on classes for breeds recognized by the organization licensing the show, and most shows also have classes for non-pedigree cats. A pedigree cat should conform to its standard of points, but non-pedigree cats are only judged on temperament and condition. However, a successful show cat should also react well in public, showing itself off: a cat that spits is unlikely to be as successful as a more relaxed cat. A cat that hates showing should not be put through the ordeal.

In order to enter your cat you must get a show schedule. Each registering body has a list of its shows and details about where to get schedules. You should also buy a copy of the relevant rules and read them thoroughly to make sure that you do not inadvertently break a rule and get your cat disqualified.

It is best to choose a local show for your first entry, preferably a small and

left: *Your cat will spend the whole day in its pen except while it is being judged. You should always provide enough comfort, food, and water.*

therefore reasonably quiet one, to introduce yourself and your cat to the show scene. GCCF shows are one-day-only events and are usually held on a Saturday, but some shows are held over two days. Write to the show manager, sending a large stamped, addressed envelope for the schedule, and study it carefully when it arrives. If you do not understand it you can telephone the show manager or ask a more experienced friend to help you complete the entry form correctly. The closing date for shows varies from a couple of weeks to a couple of months before the show, so make sure that you do not wait too long.

A show cat must be in tip-top condition, clean, and free from any signs of disease. At all GCCF shows, and many other shows worldwide, each cat is examined by a veterinarian before it is allowed into the show and

below: *What every breeder competing would like to see—reward for hard work and years of loving care. An American Chinchilla basks in the glory!*

any cat that fails this inspection is sent home or placed in a special isolation pen for the day. If your cat has fleas or dirty ears, for instance, it will be rejected, so advance preparation is essential. Your cat's vaccinations must be up to date at least a week before the show.

You must learn to groom your cat correctly for the show. For very shorthaired breeds, such as Siamese, Orientals, or Burmese, this may mean nothing more than its usual stroking, but some cats need a little extra preparation. Light-colored cats occasionally need a bath, which should be done several days before the show to allow the coat time to settle down again. Dark-colored cats may benefit from a bran bath, in which dry bran is heated in the oven then rubbed into the coat when warm, to remove any excess grease in the coat, and brushed out thoroughly. Make sure that there is nothing at

home that can stain the cat: grease, for instance, can be particularly difficult to remove and some cat litters stain the feet.

Shorthaired cats with thicker coats, such as British or Exotics, need regular brushing in any case, but may need additional grooming before a show to remove as much loose hair as possible. Semi-longhaired breeds also need scrupulous grooming to ensure that there are no tiny knots, especially underneath. Exotics and some of the semi-longhairs may also benefit from a bath before a show.

Persians need far more preparation. Their coats require daily grooming at all times, but before a show they will almost certainly need a bath to remove all grease from the coat and ensure that each hair stands out separately. In the lighter-colored cats the coat is then packed with powder that must be brushed out thoroughly until no trace remains. This helps to

above: *This Siamese is comfortable in its top-opening basket. You may also want to buy or make a draft-proof cover to use in bad weather.*

make the coats look as full and luxurious as possible. In Tabbies, on the other hand, the coat must flow but should not be fluffed out in the same way or the pattern will not be displayed properly.

The way in which Persians' coats are presented varies a little between different organizations, but wherever they are shown, correct grooming can make a tremendous difference and it is well worth attending seminars on the subject or asking experienced exhibitors how to groom a cat correctly. Under GCCF rules, no cat's coat may be clipped, trimmed, or artificially colored in any way, but correct grooming removes old coat hairs and enhances the appearance of the cat immensely.

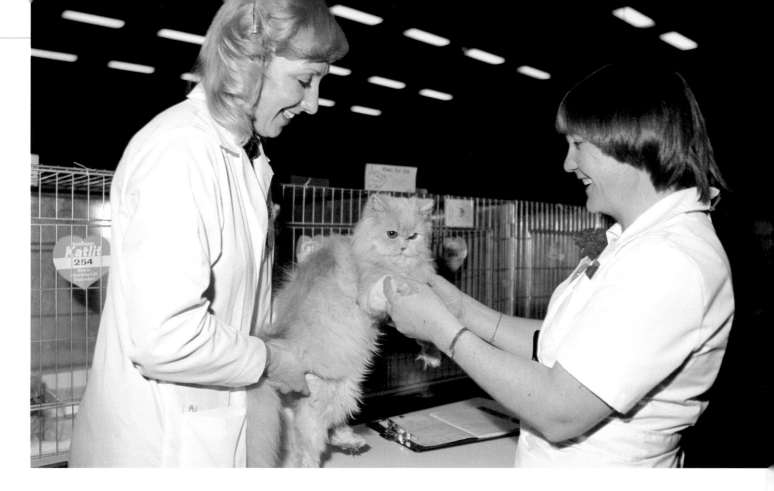

All cats' claws should be trimmed just before a show, taking great care not to cut them too short. On the morning of the show the cat should be inspected thoroughly. Any cat that is not in peak health should be left at home, even if it seemed normal the night before: a minor problem could become a major one under the additional stress of the journey and show.

On arrival at the show, after being checked-in, you need to pen your cat and make it comfortable for the day. At shows where the cats are judged in their pens, you will need to leave the pen before judging starts. Sometimes you can watch the judging from the ends of the aisles or from a balcony, but at other shows you have to leave the hall completely. You can return to your pen at lunchtime and remain there, but remember to move away if a judge approaches your cat: you must not do anything that might identify the cat. At shows where cats are taken to judging rings to be judged, you can stay by your pen all day.

When you get your results, try not to be too disappointed if your cat does not do well, or too elated if it does; the next show may give you totally different results—after all, that is part of the fun.

breeding

Cat breeding is a very enjoyable hobby, but it requires considerable thought, time, space, and expertise. You need a safe, warm place for the queen to have her litter, separate from your other cats, and you must ensure that the inquisitive kittens have a cat-safe environment.

You need to spend time taking the queen to stud and stay at home when the queen is due to kitten. If there are any problems you may need to take time off work and persuade

the family that kittens are more important than holidays.

Breeding can also be very expensive. Although kittens may be sold for high prices, this does not translate into instant profit. Even if all goes well, expenses include blood tests for the queen, stud fees, food for the queen and kittens, the kittens' vaccinations and registration fees, and any costs involved in advertising them. A healthy litter, all of which leave home before they are four months old, may give you a slight profit that can go toward the food and litter bills for the rest of the year.

However, the queen may need veterinary attention or even a cesarean, the kittens may be ill or may not leave home when expected, or you could end up with only a single live kitten to sell—or perhaps none at all. There is no guarantee that the kittens will leave home when you expect them to. This could mean half a dozen six-month-old kittens, getting bigger every day, waiting to be given away.

Even kittens that are sold may be returned for one reason or another:

left: *Burmese kittens in their playpen. Only the best kittens that are free of defects and conform well to their standard points should be used for breeding.*

above: *A pregnant cat will usually behave in normal feline fashion and should not be unduly restricted.*

they may not have settled, they may have developed a medical problem that was not obvious at the time of sale, or they may have turned out to be more trouble than the new owner expected. A responsible breeder will take these kittens back, and may need somewhere to isolate them until they can be integrated back into the family.

If you do decide to breed cats, you must select a suitable kitten. Buy a copy of the official Standard of Points and study exactly what your chosen breed should look like and which features are considered to be faults. Visit cat shows, look at the winning cats, and talk to their breeders. Be prepared to wait for what you want.

When you go to choose a kitten, take an experienced breeder with you, if you can. A breeding queen does not necessarily have to be top show quality, but she should not have any major faults, especially anatomical faults.

In all breeds the kitten should conform to the standard of points, but in some breeds the distribution of color is important on the show bench, but immaterial in a breeding queen:

the tortoiseshell pattern, for instance, is random, but some breed standards require all parts of the cat to show broken color, whereas a cat with solid-colored feet or tail is perfectly acceptable for breeding. When selecting a breeding queen, health and fertility are extremely important.

Make sure that the kitten you are thinking of buying appears perfectly healthy and inquire about its parents and grandparents. Ask about the cats in the kitten's pedigree: if several have died at an early age it could indicate a hereditary problem. Ask about the breeding history of the mother and, if known, the grandmother. You should aim to choose a kitten from a line that produces good sized litters without problems.

Before deciding to buy the kitten, ensure that she is listed on the active register. Check the pedigree and registration to make sure that the kitten is suitable for breeding the breed you wish to produce—seek advice from the appropriate breed club before buying the kitten.

Find out if there are any conditions attached to buying the kitten. It is perfectly reasonable for the breeder to insist on being informed if you have to part with the kitten, or to insist that it not be sold to a third party; most breeders are very concerned about the future welfare of the kittens they breed. Make sure that you are supplied with a properly completed pedigree, a transfer application form, and a vaccination certificate. You will need to complete the transfer application and submit it in order to transfer the ownership into your name.

While your kitten is growing up, learn more about your breed. Join the appropriate breed club, visit shows, and, if possible, attend seminars or meetings. You will need to select a stud for your queen so the more you learn and the more breeders you get to know, the better placed you will be to decide on the right stud for her.

Look at the pedigrees of the suitable studs in your area and see the cats themselves if possible. Do not pick the latest show winners, but look to their sires instead; a queen's first mating should be to an older, experienced stud with an experienced owner, since maiden queens can be difficult to mate. Ask about any conditions attached to the mating and if you are not happy with them, do not use that stud. Studs should be tested for feline

below: *Mother cat suckling her kittens. Weaning is a gradual process, the kittens learning to take some solid food while still feeding from their mother.*

leukemia and feline immunodeficiency virus and stud owners should insist that the queens also be tested, but you may not want the stud owner to have control over where you sell your kittens. Make all the arrangements well before you want to take the queen to stud, not at the last minute.

Once your queen has been mated, make a note of when she should be due to kitten—any time from 63 to 70 days later—to make sure that you will be at home. As kittening time draws close, provide her with a suitable bed; this may be a special heated bed, or simply a disposable cardboard box in a warm place, with bedding that is easy to wash. Keeping the queen in a kittening pen when you are not with her ensures that she does not choose an inappropriate place to have her kittens. Some queens, however, resent being penned up and will not settle

down to produce and rear their kittens unless they are allowed to choose their own place. Some queens are happier left alone to produce their kittens, while others like their owner with them, but all maiden (first-time breeding) queens should be watched closely for any signs of trouble.

The queen may have weak contractions on and off before settling down to kittening, but when strong contractions start there should soon be a bubble protruding from her vulva. Further contractions produce the kitten, covered in membranes and still attached to its placenta. The queen breaks the membranes, chews through the umbilical cord, and licks the kitten to dry and stimulate it.

Kittens are normally born with head and front legs first, or with tail and hind legs first; other positions, such as head or tail presented without legs,

head turned back, etc. may prevent the kitten from being born and may need correction. A placenta should accompany each kitten; a retained placenta can cause problems. If the queen does not unwrap the kitten, break the umbilical cord and dry the kitten—you must do this for her or the kitten will die. Warn your veterinarian that the queen is due to kitten and establish who you should contact in an emergency if the queen needs more help than you can provide.

A queen may produce the entire litter with little delay, or may have some kittens and settle down to feed them, waiting hours or even a day before starting contractions again to produce the rest of the litter. If contractions are unproductive, or if the queen seems unsettled but makes no attempt to produce more kittens, contact your veterinarian, as she may need help.

The queen should take care of her kittens herself until they are ready for weaning, but you may need to supplement the kittens if the queen has a very large litter. If she is ill or required a cesarean, you may need to hand-rear the kittens—both feeding and cleaning—or find a foster mother.

Kittens vary in activity: Siamese and Oriental kittens often move around their bed as soon as they are born and may start to open their eyes soon after birth, whereas Persians and British can be relatively inactive and not open their eyes until 10 days old. Early activity does not necessarily mean that the kittens can be weaned early and weaning is usually a very gradual process, the kittens learning to take some solid food while still feeding from their mother. If any kitten appears abnormal at any stage from birth onward, consult your veterinarian. The abnormality may be temporary, but if it leads to permanent impairment you need to discuss the probable outcome and consider euthanasia for severely abnormal kittens.

Consult your veterinarian about worming and vaccinating the kittens: there are different vaccine regimes, but whichever is used, the kittens should complete their vaccination course against panleukopenia and cat flu (feline viral rhinotracheitis and feline calicivirus) at least a week before leaving home.

You will also need to register the kittens and produce a pedigree for each one. Only the best kittens—sturdy, free of defects, and conforming well to their standard of points—should be used for breeding. Any kittens that are not suitable for breeding should be registered on the non-active register. Kittens on the non-active register can be shown, but only those that conform well to the Standard of Points should be sold for showing, as otherwise the new owner will be very disappointed.

Most breeders sell the majority of their kittens as pets, but you need to ensure that they are going to appropriate homes. Make sure that potential buyers know what to expect from your breed and that the kittens are being sold as pets, not for breeding, and write this on the pedigree and receipt. You may also wish to draw up an agreement that the kitten must be neutered and must be returned to you if the new owner cannot keep it.

below: *Scottish Fold—Shorthair mother with kittens. Until the weaning period the mother should have few problems, but will need more food than usual.*

glossary

Agouti Banding or ticking that produces the tabby pattern. Each hair has alternate bands of light and dark color ending in a dark point.

Awn hair Bristly hair of the undercoat. *See also* Down hair, Guard hair.

Breeches Long hair covering the top part of the hind legs.

Breed In the cat world, a type that is visibly different from its parent species, defined by shape, color, and coat quality. *See also* Family, Genus, Order, Species, Subspecies.

Breed clubs Organizations within a registry devoted to one or more particular breeds. Several clubs may exist within a registry for one breed.

Castrate Removal of a male cat's testicles. *See also* Neuter.

Cat Fancier's Association (CFA) The largest feline registry in the world, primarily based in North America; founded 1906.

Colorpoint When the face, ears, feet, and tail are darker than the rest of a cat's body. *See also* Pointed.

Down hair The insulating hair in undercoat. *See also* Awn hair, Guard hair.

Family The animals in an order that share many defining characteristics and evolutionary descent.

Feline immunodeficiency virus (FIV) Contagious to other cats, but not to humans or other animals. It is related to the HIV virus and weakens the immune system, causing death.

Feline infectious peritonitis (FIP) A disease caused by a virus, usually fatal. Symptoms include jaundice, anemia, and fluid accumulation in the abdomen.

Feline leukemia virus (FeLV) A virus affecting the lymphatic system, suppressing immunity to disease.

Feline panleukopenia A virus affecting the lining of the intestine and the bone marrow. Commonly fatal.

Feral An cat that lives wild but is descended from domestically bred stock.

FIFé Fédération Internationale Féline, an umbrella organization for European cat clubs; founded 1949.

Flehmening A method of sampling a scent using the vomeronasal organ. *See also* Vomeronasal organ.

Gene pool The total genetic diversity in a breeding group of individuals.

Genus A group of species within a family that shares characteristics and ancestry not shared by other species. *See also* Breed, Family, Order, Species, Subspecies.

Ghost markings Tabby markings, usually faint, sometimes seen in the coat of non-agouti cats or kittens.

Governing Council of the Cat Fancy (GCCF) The governing body for most British cat clubs; founded 1910.

Guard hair A waterproof layer of long, coarse hair that protects the undercoat. *See also* Awn hair, Down hair.

Hock A cat's ankle.

Jacobson's organ *See* Vomeronasal organ.

Kitten Generally, a cat below the age of nine months.

Manx A breed of cat that has no tail. The tail-lessness is caused by a gene that can cause fatal problems if passed on by both parents.

Mutation A genetic "mistake" or change from the normal state in a genetic trait.

Neuter The castration of males or spaying of females to prevent reproduction and unwanted sexual behavior.

Non-agouti A single-colored cat with no tabby markings.

Order A large group of animals with a single defining characteristic. For example carnivora; all carnivorous mammals. *See also* Breed, Family, Genus, Species, Subspecies.

Pedigree A record of a cat's ancestry, showing several previous generations.

Pointed A description of a cat's coloring when it is restricted to the extremities of the head, limbs, and tail, the body remaining pale. First known in the Siamese breed.

Queen Unspayed female cat.

Random breeding The natural process of cat breeding when cats choose their own mates without human intervention.

Recessive gene A gene that is carried but does not show itself in a cat's makeup.

Registry A national or international authority that decides on breed recognition and standards, and maintains records of pedigree breeds.

Scent marking The behavior pattern where a cat marks its territory with urine, or with scent from glands on its face, lips, and ears.

Selective breeding When humans intervene to determine the partners in any breeding.

Siamese pattern *See* Pointed.

Spay The usual method of neutering female cats, by removing ovaries and uterus. *See also* Neuter.

Species Animals sharing common ancestry and characteristics, capable of interbreeding naturally. *See also* Breed, Family, Genus, Order, Subspecies.

Subspecies A group within a species, usually created by geographic isolation, that has differences from the rest of the species but will interbreed with it where ranges overlap. *See also* Breed, Family, Genus, Order, Species.

Tabby A coat pattern developed in the wild for camouflage. *See also* Agouti.

Third eyelid A membrane that draws across the eye during sickness or following injury, concealed in the corner of a cat's eye.

TICA The International Cat Association. A registry founded in 1979, based on genetics.

Ticking Banding of light and dark colors along a hair.

Tipped Coat of light hairs with darker tips.

Tomcat Unneutered male cat.

Topcoat The outer layer of protective hairs. *See also* Guard hair.

Undercoat The insulating fur under the topcoat. *See also* Awn hair, Down hair.

Vomeronasal organ The sensory organ in the nasal cavity that analyzes smells and tastes. Also known as Jacobson's organ.

index